# NO BOSSES HERE

**Karen Brandow** has worked with alternative organizations since 1976 as a staff person, trainer, and consultant and has worked with the Citizen Involvement Training Project. Karen has also worked as a counselor and administrator in human services. She is active in the Movement for a New Society, a national network of groups working for nonviolent social change, and Re-evaluation Co-counseling, an international peer counseling network. She lives and works in Western Massachusetts.

**Jim McDonnell** has worked with Vocations for Social Change for nine years. He has been involved in all phases of VSC's work and has served as a consultant to dozens of collectives and co-ops. Jim has been involved in numerous community groups in the Mission Hill section of Boston where he has lived for the past twelve years. He has served as President of the Mission Hill Planning Commission, and is a member of the editorial collective of the Mission Hill Good News, a local community newspaper. Jim also enjoys a career as a successful little league coach.

# NO BOSSES HERE:
## A MANUAL ON WORKING COLLECTIVELY AND COOPERATIVELY

A co-publication of:
Alyson Publications, PO Box 2783, Boston, MA 02208, and
Vocations for Social Change, PO Box 211, Essex Station, Boston, MA 02112

ISBN: 0 932870 15 5    LC No. 81-68797

Co-Publishers: Vocations for Social Change and Alyson Publications

Copyeditor: Emily Hunt Nethercut

Cover Design: Marshall T. Spriggs

Typesetting: Alyson Publications

Layout and Design: Jim McDonnell, Marshall T. Spriggs, Karen Brandow, Emily Hunt Nethercut

Emotional and Material Assistance: Red Sun Press, Lucy Matson, Richard Zorza, Katie Tolles, Carol Axelrod, Mindy Friedman, and all the collectives, co-ops, organizations, and individuals who gave ideas, suggestions, and encouragement.

Publication of this book was made possible in part by grants from RESIST, and from the Boston Cambridge Ministry in Higher Education, in addition to donations from over 100 individuals and collective.

Printed in the United States by union labor.

# Contents

# INTRODUCTION

The first edition of *No Bosses Here* came out in 1976. It was written mainly for people who wanted to work in collectives, or were interested in finding out about them. So far we have sold almost 5,000 copies. The letters we've received tell us that most of the people who are reading the book are already in a collective, or are starting one. They are using it as a guide and a discussion starter.

For that reason, this new edition includes more for that audience. Most of the chapters have been expanded. We've included more about the practical skills needed to work collectively. There is also more about the theory and philosophy behind this kind of work setting.

In the past ten years, a great deal of literature has been written about alternative organizations. Many of the ideas presented here come from other places. All of these are listed in the bibliography and resource sections. These sections have also been expanded and updated.

Many of the problems of collectives come from a lack of knowledge about what other groups have done before them. Each collective tends to "reinvent the wheel." We hope *No Bosses Here* will begin to change that, and we hope to see more sharing of experiences in the future.

We welcome your reactions and comments about this book. Please write and let us know how it was helpful, and how it could be improved.

# 1. Work Collectives Today

The current growth of alternative organizations began in the sixties. People were surrounded by signs that things weren't right. They were living through and part of the Vietnam War, the civil rights movement, the 1968 Democratic Convention, the women's movement, the Kent and Jackson State killings, and several political assassinations.

One difference between the "New Left" and other social change movements in the past was that people began to see the personal as political. They were anxious and unhappy about their career choices. They saw many adults in the world's richest society leading dull and unhappy lives. They were concerned about the poor quality of relationships between family members. New Left members saw these problems as symptoms of larger social and political problems. These symptoms were the common costs of life in our society, and collective action was needed to change things. The hierarchical family, work, and learning structures in which we were raised were seen as perpetuating our separation, frustration, and boredom.

A struggle that had lain dormant since the thirties was renewed, to find new ways of living and working. Some people began by changing the institutions that already existed, such as colleges, workplaces, and the Democratic Party. Others set up new "alternative" experiments, such as co-ops, communes and collectives. People wanted to limit bureaucracy and professionalism. They wanted personal and open work relationships, and equality and democracy in their work structures. They would provide goods and services cheaply, stimulate political reforms, and restore community. This philosophy provided the initial spark for work collectives and consumer co-ops.

## Definition

Once people start having more control over their worklives, they become stronger. They see that they can influence their environment, and that they don't have to settle for whatever someone else tells them or allows them to do. This new sense of strength can carry over into the rest of their lives, their relationships, and their neighborhoods. People learn they *can* make a difference, and what they think *is* important.

What collectives are about can be summed up in the word *empowerment.* Empowerment means giving power or ability to people to control what happens to them.

### Worker Self-Management

Most collectives are owned and run by the people who work in them. The money that is made belongs to these workers. Collectives by definition want all workers to have equal input into the running of the group. Decision making is one way this happens. Many collectives use some form of consensus structure. This means everyone must feel comfortable with a decision before it is finalized. We need to be patient when we're learning democratic decision-making skills. Our society does not prepare us for democratic worklives, despite its democratic ideals. Whatever democracy our country has usually ends at the workplace.

Salaries are another area used to build in more democracy. Most collectives base salaries on equal pay for equal hours worked, or on the needs of each collective member.

People in collectives often share leadership and share skills. All skills are seen as important, and shared leadership is meant to replace hierarchy. However, some collectives find it necessary to give special responsibility for coordination to certain staff members. In any case, the structure is decided by the workers, and they can change it at any time.

### Time for Feelings

Many collective workers would say their workplace is different in a way that isn't obvious. There is a sense of warmth and unity among workers and customers that meets some basic human needs. Sometimes the quality of relationships between people is more than the relationship between sales and profits. Dan Zwerdling[1] quotes from the end of a Safeway Supermarket Annual Report, "Capital expenditures are expected to approximate $270 million." Then, from the end of a Boston Food Co-op report, "Relationships among staff members have always been more intimate than what one would expect to find in a traditional job. Staffers need to be open, to confront others with minimal emotion, and to make themselves comfortable."

Community Relations

Collectives try to provide community oriented goods and services – ones geared to people, not profits. They provide a variety of things that are usually expensive or not available at all. Child care centers, health centers, people's law offices, organizing groups, and food co-ops help working people survive. They are examples of collectives meeting people's needs. Community newspapers and radical magazines and books give news and analysis of events which aren't offered in traditional publications. Restaurants that provide a relaxing gathering place are important. Bicycle and auto repair collectives offer needed services at affordable rates. They often have programs in which they will teach people to fix their own vehicles.

View of Profits

Many collectives call themselves antiprofit. They only charge what's needed to cover their wages, overhead, and improvements to the business. Other groups do make a profit. Often such donate money to other social change or community groups. The Boston Women's Health Book Collective, authors of *Our Bodies, Ourselves* and *Ourselves and Our Children,* has given thousands of dollars to other feminist collectives.

The work of a collective is not based on making profit for individuals. Every person does have the right to a decent wage for her or his work. If the collective has more money after expenses of the collective are met and salaries paid, this money is profit. The priorities for the use of this profit should be to promote the growth of a democratic economy, and to help the struggles for social justice.

Serving as a Social Change Model

In economic terms, the collective movement across the country is tiny. But, collectives do not exist only to sell goods and services. They promote and serve as models for radical social and political change.

We live in a society that claims to be a democracy. But, we'll never have a true political democracy until we have a democratic economy. Collectives play a significant part in the struggle for a democratic economy. The creation of a work collective can be a political-social statement in itself. Collectives demonstrate that work can be done in such a way that tasks and decision making are shared, and therefore people can control their own worklives.

At Vocations for Social Change (VSC), we see communities and traditional workplaces as major fronts for social change organizing. They are the places where the oppression of working people is most obvious. Some people work for a change in traditional workplaces, helping to organize other workers. Some people get involved within their own communities, organizing such groups as tenants unions. Many of these social change efforts are run by groups organized in a collective structure.

## Cooperatives and Collectives

Collectives empower the workers through worker ownership and control. Co-ops empower consumers because they are consumer controlled. However, many collective businesses allow consumers to control some of the workplace. The Boston Food Co-op has a consumer board to set major policy. These decisions are carried out collectively by the staff, who run the co-op on a day-to-day basis. In this way, many food co-ops combine consumer and worker control. Most collectives at least have a way for consumers to voice their comments and suggestions.

This manual emphasizes collectives that charge for their goods and services and pay some salary to their workers. However, we hope that this manual will be useful to anyone interested in or involved in a collectively run social change project.

## NOTES

1. Daniel Zwerdling, *Workplace Democracy: A Guide to Workplace Ownership, Participation and Self-Management Experiments in the United States and Europe* (New York: Harper and Rowe, 1978).

# 2. Starting a Collective

There are lots of issues to look at when you start an organization. There are special problems in creating an alternative; whether it's an alternative marriage, society or business.

New groups tend to start from scratch, without looking at what others have done. Taking the time to do research, or contact other collectives could save lots of grief. Do your homework.

Often people are excited and feeling good about forming a collective. They don't anticipate problems, and they don't design ways to resolve problems. This is part of what Seymour Sarason calls the "myth of the untroubled future."[1]

It is hard to think of a collective that doesn't complain about needing more staff, money and space. Another common myth is the "myth of unlimited resources." People believe they will find as many staff as they need to provide the best possible service to all the people who need it.

Although positive thinking can be a good thing, it's possible to overdo it. As Sarason says, "The heart can make up for a lot of inadequacies, but an empty head is not one of them." New collectives must decide what their priorities are, and how they will divide up the resources they have. They must look at what they will do to help others, and what they want for themselves.

Starting a collective requires planning. Because of negative past experiences, people starting a collective often have bad feelings about the concept of planning. These feelings must be aired and dealt with from the start. The two major times for planning are when you're starting, and when you're making major changes. The rest of this chapter is about the different issues you need to consider when starting your collective. Most are discussed in detail elsewhere in this manual, as part of the ongoing work of a collective.

## What Work to Do

Collectives can do many things. In the Boston area, there are collectives involved in architecture, bicycle repair, bookselling, childcare, counseling, crafts, food, health care, law, organizing, printing, publishing, recycling, research, and woodworking. However, the possibilities are endless.

You have to choose work that can be carried out in a small, collective workplace. Collectives that try to compete with big capitalist businesses are headed for trouble. To survive competition with mass production, workers in collectives would have to work long hours at low wages. They would have no time to eat or sleep, much less to relate to each other humanly or reach out to the community. Collectives will survive politically and financially only if they form around certain skills, services and products. The most likely ones are those which are available from small workplaces in the larger society. Forget about making cars, selling life insurance, or starting a hospital.

The work you choose should also satisfy your personal and political needs. The collective will function better if you're excited by your work. We knew someone who went through three years of law school, spent over a year helping to form a law collective, and then decided that he didn't like practicing law.

The seeds for most developing collectives come from friends who work together or do similar work. This seems natural, since people doing similar work tend to become friends. Friendships can provide the initial trust and ideas from which collectives are born. Friends see a collective as a model by which they can serve the community and raise political issues.

There is much valuable information about starting a collective besides this manual. You can visit or volunteer in an existing collective. Another source is through reading and research. Appendix Five has a bibliography which lists other valuable literature.

## Goals

The Bicycle Repair Collective in Cambridge was started by several men who were dissatisfied working in straight bike shops. They felt these shops provided shoddy goods and services. They were paid low wages, even though the shops charged very high prices. Some men who worked in the same shop shared their frustrations, and hit upon the idea of starting a collective. They talked to several other friends and to other collectives. Eventually, they set up shop.

The Dorchester Law Collective in Boston started while several people were working on a prison case. They discovered they had similar interests in starting a collective. They began meeting and slowly bringing in new members. The planning process lasted a year and a half before they opened their office.

In the past, VSC has helped start many collectives. Some never got off the ground. These failed because we naively thought that if you got a bunch of people together who had the same vague sense of what they wanted to do, a collective would just happen. This turned out to be a poor formula.

To succeed, a collective needs people who share similar goals, as well as people who respect and like each other. Some questions to consider are:

- Why exactly are we getting together? What do we want to accomplish for ourselves? What "community" do we wish to serve and what do we want to accomplish for that community?
- What political goals do we have?
- What philosophy are we working from, if any?
- Do we have two sets of goals – long and short term? How long will it take to accomplish these? What are our priorities?
- What does working collectively mean to each of us?

Answering these questions is no easy task. Limit your goals. Keeping a collective's day-to-day operations going takes a lot of time and energy. Starting one requires lots of initial energy. The tendency towards a "save the world" vision can mean you get lost very quickly. Set goals that you can achieve and believe in. You'll feel better about what you're doing, and it will guard against ending your dreams in frustration.

Jaroslav Vanek has created a basic folder for starting a self-managed business.[2] One of the early steps he suggests is putting your goals and plans in writing. It's a good idea to write down everything you decide.

### Decision Making

One of the earliest and hardest issues you'll have to discuss is how you will make decisions. It's very important to be clear about this, yet many groups tend to leave it loose at the start. You may change your decision-making structure several times before arriving at what's right for your group. In the next chapter, we'll explain much more about decision making and its different forms in collectives.

## Organizational Structure

Each collective must decide on the best structure for its business or service. There is no one structure right for every group, or even for the same group through all its years. You should feel free to change the structure to meet new needs.

Most of us have had negative experiences in traditional workplaces. There is a tendency for new collectives to be antistructure. Chapter Seven explains this in more detail.

You may want to have an elected board of managers, a worker's council, or a number of coordinators. Chapter Four on dividing work gives you more options. Decide on some initial structure, and work from there.

## Bringing in Other People: Size

Once you have your goals set, and a basic idea of what the collective will look like, a next step is bringing in other people to join you. You may have specific requirements for new members, for example, that someone support feminism, or be a socialist. Whatever a group decides should be made clear to new people.

Most groups make agreement more possible by choosing new people in a certain way. The first person, or initial core group can choose the next member, that group the next, and so on. This policy doesn't mean a collective would only choose people like themselves, though that is a danger. Many collectives have chosen people of different backgrounds to have a well-rounded group. They see it as one way of working against different forms of oppression, such as racism or classism. However, it's still important to find people who have similar goals, since starting a collective is hard enough. People can become frustrated if political views are so diverse that very little work actually takes place.

Groups that function as clearinghouses can provide support in finding people for collectives. Groups like the National Lawyers Guild, Science for the People, and VSC can help.

When finding other people, you will have to deal with the issue of size. How big can you be, and still function in the way you want? Will you set a limit now, and add more people in a year once you are established? What size group is needed to accomplish your goals?

The issue of size will affect salaries. In some collectives, people have decided they would rather have a larger working group with people working different amounts of hours for different salaries than a small collective in which everyone is paid what they need. Make this decision early. It can cause problems later, and really hurt the group. At one point, the Bicycle Repair Collective had fourteen people on staff. Unfortunately, there was no way for everyone to make the income they needed from the shop. This led to lots of conflicts. After going through some painful changes, they became a four member collective.

Other collectives expect people to work at part- or full-time jobs outside the collective to make their living. They have decided they will probably never make enough money to pay everyone well. Other groups only do this as they start out, until they can pay fair salaries. You can work out whatever system suits your needs.

**Location**

How big a space do you need? Where are the people you want to serve living? What can you afford? Is there a part of town where other alternative places are located? Do you need to be very visible and obvious? All of these things will affect your decision about where your collective will be. Think this through carefully, as it can have a big influence on how successful you are.

**Legal Structure**

Before setting up shop, the IRS will want you to decide what your legal status will be. You can be a profit corporation, a nonprofit corporation, a partnership, or a worker's cooperative. In Appendix One we'll explain these options in more detail. You should find a lawyer who can help you decide what legal structure is best for you.

**Money**

Most collectives lack financial knowledge. You may want some outside help. You can talk to other area collectives. If you're in an area with few collectives, retired small businesspeople found through a local Chamber of Commerce may be helpful. They may only know about traditional businesses, but you can apply the facts to your group. If you are near a college with a business school, you may find some faculty or students can help you. Find or train someone in bookkeeping skills at the start. You need good, accurate books.

Financial decisions in a collective involve how money is raised and how it is put to use. Collectives focus on raising and using money in ways which best serve the interests of the workers and the community. Here is a list of some questions you may have to face about finances.

*Getting started.* How much money do you need to start? How should the money be used at the start? How should you raise the money? Most groups underestimate the money they'll need to start.

*Staying afloat.* Once you get going, how should you raise money to meet operating needs? How much do you need to keep going? How much of the profit should be used for salaries? How should you decide how much to pay people, and in what form (wages, benefits, dividends)?

*Meeting the future.* If you do end up with profit, how will you use it to meet the future needs of the workers and the business? Should you grow? What investments should you make now? Should you contribute to the growth of other collectives or social change groups?

Since this chapter is about starting a collective, we'll describe some of the ways collectives can get money to get going.

### Finding Resources and Money

Many collectives started with money that people had inherited or saved from other jobs. Usually one or two people would put up most of the money. The danger of this is that those people end up with more power, which leads to resentment. The person(s) with the money can always say, "Well, I don't like where the collective is headed, so I'm leaving." And there goes the financial support. If you use this method of financing, you must work carefully on issues of power that may arise.

*Loans.* These can be tricky and legally difficult. Banks are often reluctant to give loans to collectively run businesses, especially new ones.

Some individuals are willing to give interest-free or low cost loans. These are risky, since there is a chance the collective will fold and the loan won't be paid back. More often, it will be a long time before the loan can be repaid. Before taking a loan, a collective should have a realistic sense of when it can start paying the loan back, and how long it will take. People lending money should be clear about when they want the money back and whether or not they expect interest.

After many meetings and hearings, the government recently passed a bill to establish a National Consumer Cooperative Bank in Washington, D.C. The bank is a source of loans for co-ops across the country, as well as a source for other support services. The address is listed in Appendix Four. As we go to press, it is unclear what will happen with the Cooperative Bank under Reagan.

*Selling coupons.* Collective members can sell coupons to be redeemed in six months or a year. They are interest-free loans that would help a collective get started. In addition, many groups will sell coupons after they open to expand or improve their services. Several collectives in Washington, D.C. sold coupons from $2 to $10. If a collective uses this system, it must remember that the money is loaned. At some point the coupons will be traded in for goods and services.

*Selling shares.* You can become a corporation and sell shares in the community as a traditional business does. Collective members can buy at least half of the shares. People owning stock have legal control over the corporation. The issue of power would have to be thought through. To set up a corporation, a collective will need some good legal help.

*Foundations and government grants.* There are lots of books around on foundations and government grants. In your local public library, there are books on how to write proposals, and catalogues which describe and list foundations. One particularly good book is *The Grass-roots Fundraising Book*, by Joan Flanagan/The Youth Project.[3]

There are a few things to remember if you are going after grant money. Think of it as "seed money." Few places get funding for more than a few years. Try to become as self-sufficient as possible, so you aren't dependent on foundation money to survive.

Most foundations find collective work structures pretty foreign. They are used to giving money to hierarchies. At the federal level, the Small Business Administration (SBA) and the Economic Development Administration (EDA) can provide money for self-managed companies. There is a growing movement of foundations organized to provide money for social change projects. The Haymarket Foundation in Boston is one example. (See Appendix Four for other social change foundations.) A collective may have to compromise its beliefs to receive funding. Each group needs to think about this problem.

Proposal writing takes a lot of time and is often fruitless. One year, VSC sent out twenty grant proposals and received one: the grant to publish the first edition of this book. Generally, you should only write a grant proposal after visiting a funding source and after receiving assurances that you have a decent chance of receiving a grant.

*Parent organizations.* Some collectives have started with support from other organizations that have money or resources. For instance, some childcare centers and food co-ops receive free or low cost space from sympathetic churches and community organizations.

For its first five years, VSC was a program of the American Friends Service Committee. At first that meant getting free office space, and later half the budget VSC needed.

As VSC learned, there are drawbacks to this type of arrangement. The group supporting you may not be a parent in name only. They may act like some parents, especially when a group they sponsor does things that make them uncomfortable. This can create unhealthy power conflicts. You need to have an honest conversation about each other's expectations. If two groups respect each other and share political beliefs, then the arrangement has a better chance of working well.

*Creative Fundraising.* Many collectives have used techniques like bakesales, rummage sales, raffles, and canvassing in the community to raise money. These efforts make you more visible to neighborhood people. A collective can also use cultural events for benefits, such as concerts and plays. A theater company in Boston was performing the play *Working,* based on the book by Studs Terkel. VSC approached the company, and its members were happy to do a performance as a benefit for VSC. It was a chance to raise money through an event that represented VSC's feelings about issues of work in our society.

## Research

One last important task when starting a collective was mentioned at the beginning of this chapter. You should contact groups who have tried similar projects in your area and throughout the country. You can get some advice, learn from their mistakes, and make some friends in the process. You can have them send you literature about themselves, and you may want to visit some of them. Many cities have a *People's Yellow Pages* listing alternative businesses. There are resources in the appendix of this manual which you can use to find other groups.

## NOTES

1. Seymour B. Sarason, *The Creation of Settings and the Future Societies* (San Francisco: Jossey-Bass, 1972).
2. Jaroslav Vanek and Christopher Gunn, "The Basic Folder for Starting Self-Managed Businesses," in *Democracy in the Workplace: Readings on the Implementation of Self-Management in America*, ed. Ithaca Work Group (Washington, D.C.: Strongforce, Inc., 1977).
3. Joan Flanagan and The Youth Project, *The Grass Roots Fundraising Book: How to Raise Money in Your Community* (Chicago: The Swallow Press, Inc., 1977).

# 3. Decision-making and Meetings

One of the most important decisions a collective can make is how it will make decisions. Lots of factors need to be looked at. Since larger groups tend to need more structure, one factor is the size of the group. The experience level and personalities of the workers are important. The exact situation to be decided and outside pressures (like time deadlines) can also influence how decisions are made. Some questions that members of a collective might ask themselves as they think about a decision-making structure include:

- In what context do I make the decisions that I feel best about?
- What are my fears about making decisions?
- What problems do I have in listening to other people's opinions?
- What frustrates me most about meetings?

What you want to do is make the best decision in the most reasonable amount of time. The decision should be accepted by others in the group, so they will be committed to carrying it out.

**Rules of Thumb**

Here are some guidelines that many collectives have found useful.

1. Many decisions can be made by a small group. There is no sense in the whole group making every decision. But, the larger group should decide who decides. For example, supply ordering can be given to one person but the whole group decides hiring.

2. Have clear policy guidelines. That way people know when they can make decisions on their own, and when to go to the larger group.

3. Try to avoid too much or too little structure for decision making. You can find a good balance for your group.

4. Prepare as much as possible in advance for a decision; a small group can gather information or write a proposal, then bring it to the larger group.

5. Every once in a while, take time to review how decisions are made, and how people feel about decision making.

**Different Models of Decision Making**

When collectives start they often resist having any decision-making structure and prefer to just "let things happen," trusting the group to do its best. Many of these collectives are no longer with us. In Chapter Eight we will talk about the dangers of a lack of structure in collectives.

Other groups choose one method, like consensus, and think they must use it for every decision. We will describe six models here; you can use whichever method or combination of methods seems best to fit the situation. Keep in mind that if everyone agrees on the decision-making structure, then you can still be a collective.

**Autocratic (One person makes final decisions)**

Many of us know this method from traditional workplaces. It is fast, and is especially good in a crisis. If a trucker from a food co-op is handed three crates of wilting lettuce by a warehouse, it will be easier for that person to decide how to handle it, rather than calling the co-op and awaiting a group decision. On the other hand, because only one person is involved, the decision is less likely to be the best one, and is less likely to be accepted by others.

**Consultative (One person gets advice from others, then makes the final decision)**

This is a pretty fast method and involves more input than the first method. An office manager may ask others for suggestions before submitting a budget proposal, but the final choices will be hers or his. Unless trust exists, the problem still remains of a low chance of acceptance and commitment by others.

**Minority (Those with special interest make decisions)**

The lawyers in a law collective can get together and decide what kind of cases the office will accept. The big plus here is it's a decision made by experts. However, all points of view may not be heard, and this small group may not be representative of the larger one. This can work when nonexperts don't have the time or interest to pursue the issue and are willing to leave it to others. A variation on this method would be to choose a smaller but representative group to make the decision.

**Majority (Voting)**

Most of us are familiar with this style, and it can be used with any size group. However, people can get into a win/lose mentality. There is often a lack of commitment by the losers to the decision made. This can be an excellent back-up method if consensus fails.

**Unanimity (Everyone totally agrees)**

Sometimes people mistake this for consensus. It offers obvious advantages, but is almost impossible to manage with more than two people.

**Consensus (Decision made when everyone in group feels comfortable)**

A women's restaurant might use this method to decide whether or not men will be allowed to eat there. It can bring a better decision, air more opinions, and elicit more commitment. It seems to match the alternative ideology that many collectives have. But, it can take a long time, and it works best in small groups. Also, group progress can be blocked by one person, and the group may settle for the "lowest common denominator" to which everyone will agree. We'll say much more about consensus in the next section.

You may be able to think of more styles of decision making. This list shows you the range of choices. These choices may be altered too, depending on the situation.

## Consensus Decision Making

### What It Is

Consensus is a method in which all workers take an equal part in making decisions. This means that no decision is final until everyone in the group feels comfortable with the decision, and is able to implement it without resentment. Consensus relies on persuasion when there is disagreement. It's a process during which people discuss a proposal, and keep changing it to take into account different ideas or disagreements.

### What It Is Not

Consensus is not a process where you can give long speeches or tie up the group selfishly. It's not 100 percent agreement, and it should not allow pressure to settle disagreements. It isn't necessary for every person to feel that this is the solution they want most or think is best. They may feel it is the best solution that can be reached at this time under these circumstances.

### What You Need to Use It

The skill of coming to a genuine consensus is a real and hard one. The experience of many collectives suggest that at least four things are vital to using consensus successfully.

One is that all members must have equal power and information. No one person or group can be allowed to have special influence or knowledge just because they are older, stronger, wealthier, or louder. One way to achieve this equality is through job rotation, which will be discussed in the next chapter. If everyone does not have the same information, then time must be set aside to share what people need to know.

Every member must have an equal chance to debate an issue or voice an opinion before the decision is made. Some people are afraid to talk in large groups. In other groups, a handful of members may tend to dominate all discussions. The group must invent creative ways to deal with this. Some groups have a rule that no one can speak twice until everyone has spoken at least once. Others pass a cup, or some object, and only the person with the object can speak. You can break into groups of two to four to discuss the issue, and then get back together in a large group. However you do it, make sure you know where everyone stands.

Collective members must be open and honest about their feelings. People's fears can lead to subtle agreements not to talk about certain issues or problems. This can stifle and then kill a collective.

A successful collective requires commitment. Often the only thing that keeps a collective together throughout its conflicts is the conviction that the experiment of collective decision making has great value. It is hoped that value makes the pain and work worthwhile.

When making a decision, members who are in a clear minority will often be willing to give up a position when they see there is no chance to persuade other workers. This flexibility allows a collective to function, but it is not true consensus. People in the majority position need to respect the minority views. Even if the minority is one or two people, they should be encouraged to express their doubts without feeling guilty. Every proposal has its weak points, and may be improved by looking at disagreements.

Many decisions can be reversed quite easily, except for some crucial ones like hiring and firing. Everyone in the collective should keep an open mind about the success of new ideas and be willing to experiment further. More permanent decisions should be thought through more carefully so that everyone is sure that their needs are met.

One example of the consensus process was a debate at VSC about how many hours the storefront should be open for drop-in visitors. VSC had been at a low energy level, and was restructuring its program. Some collective members felt that the storefront should be open as many hours as possible to serve more people. Others wanted the storefront to be closed a lot to provide time for other work. Two members who took opposite positions were chosen by the collective to resolve the problem. It was hoped this would save time at staff meetings, which couldn't afford such tensions.

When Jim and Devon met, Jim explained his feeling that although drop-in visitors placed demands on VSC, they were one of the main reasons for VSC's existence. Devon agreed that open hours were important to VSC's work, but she wanted more quiet time to do writing and administrative work. Both agreed that when VSC was open six days a week, no one's needs were met. They decided that the storefront could be open fewer hours if they would set up counseling by appointment to serve people. Devon was excited by this idea and wanted to counsel in such a program. The idea satisfied Jim, because it would make VSC even more responsible to people who needed its services. Through this careful sharing of personal needs and ideas, the two were able to design a full week storefront schedule that excited everyone in the collective.

The Movement for a New Society has written about another example of consensus. They have seen a meeting of fifty people be ready to agree to a proposal. Then one person who hadn't been listened to at first got the group's attention through the consensus process. He persuaded the whole group to decide differently. Everyone agreed that the new decision was wiser. In a voting situation, a person outnumbered so heavily might feel that the situation is hopeless, and give up.

A Sample Process for Consensus

Your group can decide what works best for you when making consensus decisions. A basic outline is suggested below, and you can vary it in whatever way makes sense for you.

• First you must agree on what the issue or problem is. This sounds simple, but sometimes discussions can drag on because people are seeing the problem in different ways.

• You can give each person two or three minutes without comment or interruption to state their feelings or ideas about the issue. Listen for agreement and hesitations.

• If there seems to be general agreement, state what you hear in the form of a question, like "Do we all agree that we'll meet on Tuesday evenings for the next two months, and that at each meeting we'll find a facilitator for the next one?" Insist on a response from people, and don't assume that silence means agreement.

• If there is no agreement, ask those who disagree to state their objections. There are several choices at this point.

a. Propose a break or period of silence to think.

b. Change the proposal so the objections are taken into account.

c. People who felt one way may be convinced to the minority view.

d. A new proposal can be made.

e. Postpone the decision. If you do this, it may help to have people from opposing sides work together to come up with a compromise as illustrated in the example involving Jim and Devon.

f. If one or two people are blocking consensus, remember you cannot override them – they must override themselves. They can allow the group's needs to be more important than their own. Sometimes they can clearly state their opinions, and allow the group to go on in the interest of time. It will help if the group records the lack of unity in the minutes, and agrees to reconsider the decision after a trial period.

g. As a last resort, every group can have a back-up plan if they don't reach consensus in a certain amount of time, such as 75 percent voting for a decision. Remember to record all decisions made by the group.

**Summary**

Below is a list of the basic points we've made about decision making. You will be the final judge of what works best in your group.

What Works

- defining the group that will make the decision
- defining when the decision is made and recording it
- separating policy decisions from day-to-day worklife decisions
- using consensus in groups in which there is basic trust and commitment
- using small task forces to make decisions to bring to the large group
- giving the necessary information to everyone involved in the decision
- dealing openly with problems between people
- agreeing on what would make you reconsider a decision
- tabling a decision when necessary
- agreeing ahead of time on what to do if consensus doesn't work

What Does Not Work

- having everyone take part in every decision (especially in large groups)
- forcing consensus in large groups whose members do not basically agree or know each other
- making decisions without adequate information
- avoiding tough ideas or decisions
- deciding without defining the problem (everyone solving her or his own concept of the problem)
- failing to clearly say how a decision will be implemented
- making important decisions when tired

**Problems in Decision Making**

Earlier in this chapter we mentioned four vital factors in making consensus work. Problems arise if group members lack equal power, do not have equal chances to discuss issues, are not open to feelings, or lack commitment. Many of us are used to relying on others to make decisions. It can be hard to take that responsibility upon ourselves. It is natural to find that collectives have to struggle against the assertion of power by some members, and the refusal to take responsibility by others. This is partly an interpersonal issue. But there are also changes in the structure that can help a collective.

Often, for example, some members in the collective gain more power. This is not always because they are power hungry, but because the outside world sees them as the key people in the collective, and always turns to them for information.

The Haymarket People's Fund is a collectively run foundation that funds community organizing efforts in New England. One person who started the organization had become associated with it in the minds of the community. (It did not make it any easier that his family name is displayed on the shelves of your local supermarket.) This person and the collective realized that because people recognized his name, people who called always asked for him. This was creating a power hierarchy. They decided that the issue needed dealing with. They wrote a long article in the foundation newsletter explaining the problem and asking people to please deal with whomever answered the phone at Haymarket instead of asking for the "heavy."

Since many of the people who work in collectives have been badly burned in traditional jobs, they want a collective to offer security. Providing support is one of the great strengths of a collective. This means, however, that people need to learn not only how to insist that they not be pushed around, but also how to make exciting decisions. Often people veto decisions which they find personally threatening. Since collectives often use consensus, the insecurity that comes from the pain of working in hierarchies can make for conservative decisions.

Sometimes collectives get into a habit of avoiding difficult issues. As these issues are confronted and worked through, people can gain confidence and feel safer in the group. For controversial issues to be resolved, people in a collective need to start with a basic agreement on goals and political philosophy. If differences are too great for progress, ultimately someone will have to leave the collective. This is not always a disaster; it can release lots of creativity.

Decision making in a collective is not easy. In many ways it requires more thought and energy than voting on everything or having one person decide everything. Remember, it takes time for a group to work together well. The world is not going to end if your group makes a mistake.

### Meetings, Agendas and Facilitation

Paul Bernstein and Lew Bowers have written, "The world is run by those who stay to the end of meetings."[1] This may be true, but meetings can be overused in a collective, so you should be sure there is a clear reason to have one. Meetings are an important part of working for social change. They are times to share information, make decisions, give each other support, and accomplish tasks. It's probably best to set aside separate meetings for political discussions, socializing, or dealing with feelings. If clear time is set aside for such issues, people will respect decision-making time and focus on the business at hand.

How long and how often you meet is up to you. VSC has had anywhere from two meetings a month to four a week. One collective we know endured weekly seven hour meetings where all issues were talked through and decided upon. Most collectives meet once a week for two to three hours. The most effective meetings occur when everyone is clear on what the meeting is about, when people have prepared for the meeting, and the group has a facilitator, or chairperson.

### The Agenda

Here are some tips on forming an agenda for a meeting.

- Have the agenda set ahead of time. Many groups post a sheet of paper on the wall during the week where people can write in issues as they come to mind.
- Give each person in the meeting a copy of the agenda, or have it posted so everyone can see it.
- If people can do any premeeting work on an item, have them do it.
- Separate quickly accomplished items and announcements from longer discussions.
- Prioritize agenda items and set time limits on each.
- Make sure the group accepts the agenda.

### The Role of the Facilitator/Chairperson

Many of us learn to facilitate or chair a meeting through experience, or by watching others. We can learn from mistakes and from good and bad meetings. Many collectives like to give everyone a chance to run meetings. They may rotate this job each week or once a month. That person has a major responsibility, and some of their tasks will be explained later.

A facilitator never directs the group without its consent. She or he helps the members of a group decide what they want to do in a meeting, and helps them carry it out. A good facilitator helps people be aware that *they* are in charge, and that it is *their* business that is being handled. A facilitator should try to draw out the leadership skills and potential of all group members. One need not be labeled "facilitator" to use these skills in a group. Anyone can give feedback, interrupt conflict, or get a group back on track. As we all develop these skills, less and less of the chore of running a meeting will fall on the facilitator alone. There are some things the facilitator can do to prepare for the meeting:

• get the space ready: arrange chairs, make sure people can hear, make the room comfortable.

• gather materials: get copies of the agenda, paper, pencils and pens, an easel or blackboard, chalk or magic markers.

• make sure that everyone knows when and where the meeting is.

• think of ways a complex or tension-producing agenda item can be made easier to deal with.

Running the Meeting

Once the meeting is set up, the facilitator can follow some or all of these guidelines:

1. Start on time – otherwise you end up punishing those who do come on time.

2. Give everyone a minute or two to say how they're doing, so people can be aware of any outside tensions that might affect someone in a meeting.

3. Review the agenda and get it approved, added to, or corrected.

4. Assign someone to take notes. Minutes should at least include a list of who was there, a record of every decision made, any responsibilities that were taken and by whom, and any announcements that were made. This is helpful for follow through, and for filling in group members who were absent.

5. Assign someone to keep track of time if it will help you.

6. Appoint someone who will not participate in the meeting, but who will observe the "group process" and report what they see. Chapter Five explores more about the role of this person.

7. Use short items, fun activities, and breaks to give a rest from hard decision making.

8. Keep the role of the chair neutral. If you offer personal opinions, make sure people know you're speaking for yourself and not as the chairperson. If you get deeply involved in something, assign another person to facilitate for that time.

9. Go through the agenda item by item.

a. Give people two to three minutes to think quietly on a new item.

b. Ask for proposals, bring out opinions, encourage various viewpoints. Expect differences of opinions; they lead to creative solutions.

c. Help make it comfortable for everyone to participate; break into small groups if the group is large.

d. Identify issues, restate ideas, clarify. Ask the group, "Where are we now?"

e. Be suspicious of agreements reached too easily; check these decisions out.

f. Keep the conversation on the topic; point out when it drifts off. Keep people responding to what was just said, and remind people that they don't need to talk if they have nothing to add.

g. Don't let discussion continue between two people; ask for comments by others.

h. Try to make people speak for themselves only, and to be specific when they are referring to other people.

i. Point out interpersonal problems you see arising.

j. Keep looking for minor points of agreement and state them. This helps keep up morale.

k. Check for consensus on items.

10. Select a facilitator for the next meeting, and a time and place.

11. Take at least fifteen minutes to do an evaluation of the meeting. Some collectives use the techniques of criticism/self-criticism explained by Gracie Lyons (see Appendix Five).

12. End on time as a reward for hard work.

Following a procedure like this will, we hope, make meetings less dreadful to people in collectives, and more productive and fun. This list may seem regimented, but in time these behaviors become more natural. An excellent resource for information about decision making and meetings is the Movement for a New Society, which is listed in the appendix.

## NOTES

1. Paul Bernstein and Lew Bowers, "Democratic Organizing and Management," *Communities* (29), 1977: 26-39.

# 4. Dividing Collective Work

Every collective needs to decide how it is going to divide up the work that has to be done. Who would do what, at what times, and according to what standards? Collective work means shared responsibility, and an equal chance to learn new skills and teach old ones. You can be informal or structured about how work is to be done. Some collectives divide work by members' interests, others by people's skills or formal credentials. But all collectives try to give people an equal chance to grow and do interesting work.

**Skills and Skill-Sharing**

Everyone has valuable skills to offer. In most traditional workplaces skills and credentials make some people more powerful than others. If we can learn these skills from each other, we can develop leadership skills in more people.

Some people fear that the collective's product or service won't be as good if the work is shared. We must find ways to train the unskilled, while keeping the quality of our work high.

Some skills are easier to share than others. Mechanical tasks seem easiest to share, since all that's usually required is memory, patience, and coordination. The same is true of repetitive work like typing and filing. The problems of tedious and hard work are different from those of exciting and interesting work. Everyone should be willing to do both. Earthworm is a group that does environmental education and runs a recycling business. Staff are paid for doing educational work and for work "on the truck." At a Western Massachusetts law collective, everyone did her or his own typing, unless a brief was needed that had to be typed quickly and neatly. In general, collectives try to arrange for rote work to be shared by everyone.

Other skills are harder to share, like writing, public speaking, and fundraising. Many people are angry and hurt about not being taught these things in their schooling and elsewhere. As with all skill-sharing, the key is personal support and good planning.

Then there is a set of skills that only certain "professionals" learn, and these are hardest to share. Obvious examples are law and medicine. For example, usually only lawyers can plead in court. So, some law collectives have set up groups of lawyers and laypeople to work on cases together, until the case goes to court.

Fortunately there is a growing movement to make medicine and legal information more available to everyone. We hope this will mean we won't have to rely so much on professionals in the future.

## Models of Work Structure

As collectives have evolved, they have come up with a variety of ways to divide work. Here are some methods that are most often used.

### The Whole Collective Takes Responsibility

This was the early basic collective idea. Take for example, the distribution of VSC's second *People's Yellow Pages*. No one person wanted to handle the distribution, since no one enjoyed it. So, the collective decided that everyone would share the work. First, there was a list of bookstores made up from the "capitalist" *Yellow Pages*. Then there was a discussion of how to approach a store manager. It was agreed that the best way was to go in person with publicity materials. Someone prepared the materials in draft form. They were changed and approved by the whole group, and then someone had them printed. People agreed to go in pairs to the bookstores. This method works well when there is a large task that no one wants to do or when a new collective wants to develop trust and support.

The second *People's Yellow Pages* would never have been widely distributed without this process. But there were drawbacks. Such large group work can be very time consuming. It can be counter-productive for everyone to talk endlessly over every detail of every project. As collectives become more experienced and as the trust level rises, groups develop other ways of handling problems at work.

Short-Term Work Groups

For later editions of the *People's Yellow Pages*, a smaller group of staff brainstormed and designed the distribution system. Everyone in the collective was still responsible for going to bookstores, since no one liked this task. However, the planning time was reduced.

Rotation of Jobs

This is a standard technique used in almost every collective. There are always unpopular tasks, from sweeping the floor to answering the mail or keeping books. Rotating these jobs is one way to deal with this problem. Each person would take his or her turn to be janitor of the week or bookkeeper of the year, or whatever. When the task is complicated, it's easier to have two people do it at a time, with one rotating off and being replaced by a novice halfway through the time period. This means everyone is in training half-the-time, and is the "expert" for the other half. Bookkeeping is often handled in this way.

Job wheels are another technique that makes rotation clearer. All the unpleasant jobs are listed on the outside of a cardboard wheel, and people's names are put on a smaller wheel that is pinned inside. The inside wheel is moved one spot each day, week or month. This means each person gets to do one unpleasant task at a time. Then everyone knows who to yell at when the garbage piles up!

Work Days

Another way of getting work that no one wants to do out of the way is to set up a special work time. At VSC we set up special work times to update the library, to work on a publication or to do bulk mailings. Other groups will set aside a day when the office is closed, and everyone comes in to clean up the space – washing walls, cleaning out file cabinets, etc.

Permanent Work Groups

Often collectives will set up more permanent small work groups that are responsible for a specific program or area of work. In some collectives, the bulk of the work is carried by these small groups. VSC has had groups responsible for one-to-one counseling, the unemployment law project, and the labor information project. These groups coordinate the work of the project and make minor decisions. All major decisions are brought before the whole collective. Each group gives regular reports on their work at staff meetings. At this time, suggestions, support, and criticism are offered. Disagreements are worked through the collective as a whole.

Specialization

Food co-ops are an example of a method of collective organization which we call specialization. Some food co-op stores have specialists in grains, groceries, produce, and dairy goods. Each specialist is responsible for the ordering, display, delivery, and accounting of their area. They also coordinate the work of members in their area. (Most co-ops require members to work several hours a month to keep expenses and prices low.) Other co-ops use people according to general tasks. There are floor managers, a bookkeeper, and an ordering person.

Specialization can be helpful when there is a day-to-day flow of information and lots of small decisions that have to be made. If you use this method, be sure that everyone shares in some enjoyable work as well as the tedious work.

Volunteers

Many collectives use volunteers to help with their work. This can be valuable for all involved. The volunteer learns skills and the collective gets its work done while enjoying the input of a new person. There can be problems with volunteers, which we'll discuss later in this manual.

## How to Decide

Collective organization involves many choices. Will the work be done quickly, or is skill-sharing to be the priority? Which project is most important, and what does it require? Should there be lots of interpersonal support, or would a very close group be restrictive? People need to sort through these issues when deciding how to structure their work.

Decisions about structure should improve worker control. Every collective must decide for itself what the group needs in order to function best. Here are some questions the group can consider.

- What political and economic beliefs does the collective want its work to express?
- How do members of the collective like to work? What did they like most about their past work experiences? What do they want to avoid?
- Can the demands of the work itself best be met by individuals

or groups?

- How can people best use the skills they have?
- How can we make sure that a few people don't end up with all the power?
- What decisions can be made by subgroups or individuals?
- How do we create an atmosphere for supportive teaching and learning, while still making sure the work gets done?

People can also ask themselves what skills they have to offer, how they want to use those skills, and what skills they want to learn in the group.

## If You Run Into Problems

If problems arise in a given task, do not jump on the person(s) involved and assume the fault lies with them. Perhaps the task itself is too large or impossible. Maybe more people should help or the task should be divided. It could be the person lacks the information necessary to do the task. The group's expectations may not match those of the person doing the job. You might write a clear job description as a solution to this. Maybe the person is not suited to the job. They may need more training, more support or more criticism. Perhaps that person is better suited for another task. The point is, take a closer look to see what's really happening when work isn't being done.

## Change and Flexibility

Changes in the work structure of a collective occur all the time. People's needs and skills change, and the work changes. The structure must acknowledge that people are different, and that people change over time.

In some cases a new collective starts off with everybody doing everything. As people become more confident and develop new interests, the structure changes. As the work becomes more clear and people more trusting, the work becomes divided in a fair manner. Other groups go through a different pattern. Some workplaces start as traditional businesses, and decide to change to a collective as people explore skill-sharing.

Sometimes changes take place when there is a lot of stress and extra work. In the early days of VSC, it was a matter of principle that everyone be able to do everything. That was in reaction to the hierarchical division of labor that most members had worked under before. Many jobs were left to be done when people felt like doing them (if ever). When the collective was putting together the third *People's Yellow Pages* some members preferred to specialize in counseling and storefront work while others worked on the publication. People realized that this specialization was not a "defeat" for the collective process but an improvement in the structure of work. It then became important for each group to keep the other informed of its work and its needs for support. The structure allowed people to grow in the work they cared most about without being excluded from other things that were important to them. The decision to allow for this specialization also meant that the collective had to become much more deliberate about seeing that all tasks got done.

## Conclusion

How a collective organizes its work is as important as what work is done. Traditional workplaces tend to foster competition, isolation, hierarchy, and stagnation. Collectives challenge those traditions by exploring alternative ways of working together on a day-to-day basis. This is another important contribution they make towards building a better society.

# 5. Group Dynamics

Group dynamics is the study of how people function together in groups. There are thousands of books written on the topic, concerning groups of every kind. You don't have to be an expert on groups to have a good experience in a group. There are some basic, practical ideas and skills that can help your group be more effective. This information can help you understand what is happening, and what to do about problems. In this chapter we'll present some basics about what to observe in a group, and a well known theory of group development.

**Complexity**

In many ways, groups are harder to make sense of than individuals. There is a lot going on at once, and a group is truly more than the sum of its parts. When you are trying to understand what is happening, you can look at it in a variety of ways.

Let's say that Anne is not assertive at meetings. We could say that's because she got punished by her parents for talking at the dinner table when she was young, so she's afraid to speak up. Or we could say the person facilitating the meeting may not like her, and won't call on her. We could notice that the norm in the group is that people interrupt each other a lot, which makes it harder for Anne to say what's on her mind. Finally, we could notice that women in our society are not encouraged to be assertive, and the "real problem" lies there. Any one or all of these ideas may be right.

**What to Observe in a Group**

When people interact, there are two things going on. One is that they are talking *about* something, or working on some task. That is called the "content." Most of the time, this is the only thing people pay attention to. When we examine *how* the group is working, and what is going on between people, that is called "process." If you can become aware of group process, you can diagnose group problems early and deal with them more effectively. Here is a list of guidelines to help you look at group behavior.

Communication/Participation

- Who talks? For how long? How often?
- Who interrupts whom? Who talks after whom?
- Who talks to whom? Do you see a reason for this?
- Is there a time quiet people become talkative, or talkative people become quiet? When does that seem to happen?
- How are silent people treated? How is their silence interpreted?

Influence

This is not the same as participation. Some people say little but get the group's attention. Others say a lot but aren't listened to.

- Which people are listened to when they talk? How can you tell?
- Who isn't listened to? Do you see any reason for this?
- Are people fighting for leadership? How is this affecting other group members?
- In what way do people try to influence each other?
    - Do they try to impose their will, judge others or block action?
    - Do they try to avoid conflict and leave decisions to others?
    - Do they get attention by being uninvolved and uncommitted?
    - Do they try to include everyone by being open with feelings?

Decision Making

Groups are making decisions all the time, even when they don't realize it. Seeing how decisions are made, and if the group is doing what it wants is important. Group decisions can be hard to undo later, when you're implementing the decisions. When someone says, "Well, we decided it, didn't we?" fighting back gets hard. However, other problems arise when people always want to reverse decisions or forget decisions were made. It helps to look back and see how the decision was made, and if that method was appropriate.

- Does a majority push a decision through over objections?
- Does the group jump from topic to topic? What are the reasons for this?
- Is there an attempt to get everyone involved in the decision?
- Does anyone say something that gets ignored? How does this affect that person and others?

Atmosphere

We are all brought up to be competitive. Sometimes there is more conflict and disagreement in groups than necessary. Some people may seem to prefer conflict, while others are afraid of it.

- Who seems to push for a friendly atmosphere? Is there an attempt to suppress conflict or unpleasant feelings?
- Who seems to disagree constantly? Does that person annoy or provoke other group members?
- Are people involved and interested? Are they working, playing, bored?
- Are there any subgroups? Sometimes two or three members may constantly agree with and support each other. Sometimes they disagree with and oppose whatever the other says.
- Do some people seem "outside" the group? Are others "in"? How are the "outsiders" treated?
- Do people move in an out of the group? When?

Nonverbal Dynamics

Sometimes we can overdo it with interpretations, but other times how people communicate without talking can be important. These are some things you can watch for.

- Who sits where? Where are they in relation to each other?
- How are people sitting – slouched, legs crossed, head down?
- Who looks at whom during a meeting?
- When do people smoke, if allowed? Are glasses put on and taken off?
- Is silence allowed? What role does it play?
- What expressions are on people's faces?
- Does the way people look match what they are saying?

Norms

Most groups develop ground rules about how people should or should not behave. These are called norms. If everyone knows what the norms are, they are clear or explicit. If the norms aren't talked about directly they are unclear or implicit. These norms can help or hurt group progress.

- Are certain topics avoided, such as talking about feelings or sexual attractions between members? Why and how do people avoid these topics?
- Are people too nice to each other, or do they disagree too easily?
- Do people talk using a certain jargon or language with each other?

Social Issues

All the areas discussed above can be observed to see if there are problems created by sex, class, race, or age differences. For instance, does it seem that men talk more, even if there are an equal number of men and women? Do only women discuss feelings? Do people not listen when a working-class person speaks? At a drop-in counseling center we know of, it was noticed that new points or suggested actions raised by women were only acted on when a man in the group repeated the idea.

Obviously there is a lot to observe in a group. You can't pay attention to all of these areas at once. You can assign someone to watch a meeting with one or two issues in mind, and report to you at the end as to what he or she saw. As you notice things during the meeting, you can point them out. Try to report just what you see, without adding a long socio-political analysis. This is especially important when you're first learning group process, since it can take a while for people to trust someone watching them closely.

You may want to set up some new rules if unhelpful things are going on in the group. Sometimes, just bringing them to people's attention can make them change.

## Two Functions in Groups

To have a successful group, two needs must be met; what it takes to do the job and what it takes to strengthen and build the group. People take on roles in a group to make sure both needs are addressed. As you read through the lists below, you can think about who in your group does what. You can identify and fill unfilled roles. You can become more aware of what you might do to make the group run smoothly.

Roles that Help Set and Meet Goals

- Initiating: suggesting new ideas, proposing goals, defining problems.
- Seeking information: requesting facts, asking for clear

suggestions.

- Giving information: offering facts, relating experiences to group problems.
- Seeking opinions: asking for feelings or opinions from others.
- Giving opinions: stating feelings or beliefs, evaluating an idea.
- Elaborating: giving examples, developing meanings, explaining.
- Coordinating: showing how ideas are related, pulling together activities of subgroups.
- Summarizing: offering conclusions, pulling together issues.

Roles Needed to Keep Group Harmony

- Encouraging: being friendly and warm, praising others' ideas.
- Gatekeeping: making it possible for everyone to talk. For example, the chair might point out, "We haven't heard from Jorge yet," or "Each person should have two minutes to speak."
- Standard setting: showing the group when decisions conflict with group norms, suggesting new norms.
- Listening and following: going along with group decisions, paraphrasing what someone has said.
- Expressing feelings: saying how you feel, restating others' feelings.
- Compromising: admitting mistakes, offering or accepting a compromise.
- Relieving tension: joking, suggesting breaks, putting a tense situation in a wider context.

Roles that Help with Goal Setting *and* Group Harmony

- Evaluating: diagnosing problems, noting progress and blocks, showing what steps to take next.
- Testing for agreement: stating agreements, making proposals for group reaction.
- Harmonizing/mediating: helping solve conflicts, offering compromises.

From time to time, people behave in ways that do not help and may harm the group. Some of the common ways are listed here.

Behaviors that Hinder the Group

- Being overly aggressive: working for status by criticizing or blaming others, being hostile.
- Blocking: going off on tangents, arguing too much on a point, rejecting ideas without consideration.
- Competing: vying with others to talk the most, and offer the

best ideas.

- Seeking sympathy: trying to get support by putting your own ideas or yourself down.
- Horsing around: clowning, mimicking, disrupting the work of the group.
- Seeking recognition: drawing attention by talking loudly, coming up with extreme ideas, or behaving wierdly.
- Withdrawing: daydreaming, doodling, whispering to others, leaving, acting passively.

## A Theory of Group Development

Most researchers have found that groups have a life of their own. Like people, they seem to go through different phases. There are many theories that describe these stages. William Shutz proposes a clear, widely used theory with three stages.[1] These stages are based on three needs that people have.

Inclusion

The concern here is "Where do I fit." Group members are dealing with questions like "How much of myself will I devote to this group?" "How important will I be here?" "Will they appreciate who I am and what I can do?" As individuals are sorting out their positions, the group as a whole is defining its goals and ideals. As described in Chapter Two, people are examining what work the collective will do, and what the philosophy of the collective will be.

Once the group gets going and people begin to feel comfortable, the next phase begins.

Influence

In this phase, people ask themselves questions like, "How much influence do I want to have with people here?" "How much will I let others influence me?" "How much responsibility will I take and how much will I let others have?" During this stage, there may be struggles for leadership, fights, and competition. We hope that through the process of resolving conflicts and going through hard times, people begin to feel closer. Then the group moves on to the final phase.

Affection

Anxieties may arise about not being liked or not being close enough to others. Some people may fear that they are too intimate. The group may go through a "honeymoon period" where everything is wonderful. Members can pair off and become jealous, or express lots of positive feelings for each other. They have fun together, too.

Keep in mind that the group as a whole doesn't move from one stage to the next. Some people can get stuck in one stage; others may be quick to settle one set of issues, and move on to the next ahead of everyone else. Inclusion is the stage at which new people start no matter what stage other people are at.

Also, the group does not reach affection and stay there. The group repeats this cycle over and over, and each time maybe in more depth. When people leave the cycle is reversed. First, people tend to break their affectionate ties, then they become less concerned with the issue of influence, and finally they don't participate at all.

This theory can be useful for understanding what is going on in your group. It could help you decide what should be done to resolve problems. For instance, if you notice that new members of the collective have poor attendance records and tend to show up late at meetings, they may be telling you that they feel excluded. You can set aside some time to let them know they are welcome in a variety of ways.

There are many techniques for dealing with the process issues. It can be hard to work out these issues on your own. If problems persist, it might be a good time to call in an outside facilitator.

## NOTES

1. William Schutz, *Elements of Encounter*, (Big Sur, CA: Joy Press, 1973).

# 6. Dealing with Feelings

At their best, collectives are places where people can grow and develop their personal strengths. Learning to handle conflicts and improve relationships are important parts of a collective's existence. Growth requires us to be open, to believe in our strengths, to understand our weaknesses, and to look at how we interact with others.

Most of us grew up believing that expressing feelings was not okay. Yet feelings will come up all the time when we work with others. Our goal is to find constructive and safe ways to deal with those feelings. Relationships between people can be a great source of support, learning, and cooperation. When relationships break down, they can lead to tension, conflict, and disruption.

## Times and Settings for Feelings

Meetings

Some collectives set a time at the end of each staff meeting to discuss feelings. The group looks at how the meeting went, and how people are getting along. Other groups prefer to raise those issues as they arise during the meeting. When things are left to the end, tensions can build up and interfere with the progress of the meeting. On the other hand, you could get stuck dealing with interpersonal conflicts and never get to the rest of the agenda. It can help to set time limits on all issues; business and interpersonal. If there seems to be a lot of interpersonal issues not being dealt with, you can set aside time for a special meeting.

Feedback Meetings

Some groups use a regular meeting to deal with interpersonal issues. They look at conflicts, and look at the positive and negative ways that people are working together. When VSC became a larger collective, staff members realized that staff meetings were becoming longer and that there was more tension. No one knew how or when to deal with interpersonal issues. This meant that some conflicts were bottled up while others spilled over all the time, disrupting the work process. So, VSC decided to have weekly (later, biweekly) meetings to handle these tensions.

Examples of issues that came up were competition between people, someone's tendency to overwork, and a member's problem in a personal relationship that was causing him not to be his usual productive self.

At the start of each feedback meeting, each person said whether he or she had an issue for the group to discuss, and gave a rough guess as to how much time was wanted. We tried to keep the meeting to two hours. (Two hours is the collectively agreed upon fade-out time.) The chairperson for the meeting would add up the time everyone asked for, and through negotiating time the agenda would be agreed upon. For example, some things could wait till next week, some could not. Flexibility is the key, since you don't want to cut off people discussing an important personal issue.

As VSC became a smaller collective, interpersonal conflicts were handled in more one-to-one talks, or as part of the agenda of a regular staff meeting. We worked hard at giving each other a lot of appreciation and praise for our work and our work relationships. When we had a hard time dealing with issues, we used a skilled outside person to help us out. This helped immensely.

### Retreats

Many groups have regular retreats. They go away for a weekend in order to deal with interpersonal issues. Obviously, retreats can be used for dealing with any kind of issue. Retreats should be planned. If there are some tough issues to be resolved, you may wish to use an outside facilitator.

You can combine issues. One such weekend might devote half-a-day to political direction (perhaps with some reading in advance), half-a-day to dealing with interpersonal problems in the group, half-a-day to future concrete planning, and half-a-day to collective sunbathing. Other issues could include women's workstyles/men's workstyles, or class and race issues. There are exercises and role plays you can use to help you work on issues. The bibliography in

Appendix Five has some literature that can help.

Some people think a retreat is impossible, because there is so much work to do, and not enough time. These people need to understand that the quality of work will suffer if the personal issues are ignored. There are many inexpensive retreat centers run by progressive groups.

Using a Third Person to Help

In conflicts between more than two people, or in which there are lots of intense feelings, you may want to ask another person to help with the discussion. If you want to do this, ask someone you all trust, who can stay neutral and not take sides. Be clear about exactly what kind of help you want from this person, and speak up if they aren't giving you what you need.

There are several roles a third party can play. A third party can help people vent feelings, raise questions and clarify issues, suggest processes for resolving conflicts, make sure each side is really listening to the other, or silently observe and report observations at the end. Make sure you all agree about what the third party is to do and not do.

## Guidelines for Feedback

Giving constructive criticism and praise is a skill we don't get much chance to learn. There are lots of guidelines you can keep in mind, some of which you are familiar with already through common sense. For example, if Mitch has some criticism to give Nancy, he should consider these things.

- Has Nancy asked for the feedback? If not, is she willing to listen and work it out?
- He should focus on Nancy's behavior, and not his interpretation of it. "You complain frequently," not "You're immature."
- He should say something specific, not general. "You often come late to meetings," not "You don't follow through on commitments."
- Why is Mitch telling Nancy this? Is it to help her to make some change in her behavior, or just to vent his own feelings? He should tell her which.
- Try not to assume blame. We are all living with enough guilt. Chances are Nancy has raked herself over the coals for her constant complaining and feels vulnerable about it. This is another reason why Mitch should try to be helpful and supportive in his criticism.

• Is this a good time for Nancy to hear what Mitch has to say? If other people are around, or if she seems involved in her work, he may want to ask for a time to get together.

• How much will he say? We sometimes tend to overdo it when learning to give feedback. It's as if Mitch is saying, "I just happened to have a list of reactions here, so if you'll settle back for a few hours, I'll read them off to you." (Don't laugh – we've seen this done!) Nancy can only take in so much at once.

• Is Mitch's feedback about something that happened recently? If so, Nancy will remember it better. Mitch should try to avoid letting bad feelings build up or he may lose his temper in a destructive manner.

There are some things Nancy can keep in mind when hearing Mitch.

• If she wants to hear something from Mitch in particular, she can ask.

• Nancy should make sure she understands what Mitch is saying. A common and inappropriate response is, "Well, I don't like the way you..." One-upping is not helpful and is hard to avoid. Deal with criticisms one at a time. The idea is to help each other, not hurt each other.

• She can share her reactions with Mitch, even if she has lots of feelings. A reaction such as, "Well, I hear what you say and I'll change" may be burying a lot of emotions. It's fine for her to say "I feel really defensive now, but I want to work on this and improve our relationship. One way you might help me is to..." If Mitch doesn't know her reaction, he may be less apt to give her feedback in the future.

## Problems of Collective Work

### Feeling Included

It is not easy for a new person to join a collective. Members may know each other well and have set ways of relating. New people can feel like outsiders. They don't have a history or information about the group that other people have. The same may be true for part-time workers and volunteers. They aren't accepted as being part of the group.

Collectives can plan ways to involve these people. Such planning includes introducing people to the day-to-day operation of the collective; the accounts, the history, the ways of making decisions.

A formal orientation session is one way to do this. Or, each "veteran" could spend time with a new person, covering a different aspect of the collective. This method allows new people a chance to meet their coworkers on a one-to-one basis and can be a nice way to begin to make someone feel part of the group. For skill-sharing, a new person can be paired with an old member as an apprentice. She or he can slowly take on more responsibility as the job is learned. Whatever the method, you should have a clear way of integrating new people into the collective, whether they be volunteers or staff people. Social gatherings are a good informal way of helping make people feel part of the group.

### Issues of Power and Control

As in life, these may be the biggest issues collectives have to deal with. People join collectives or form collectives because they want more control over their worklife. But, people must give up some of their independence for the group to function cooperatively. Ideally, we are trying to blend meeting individual and group needs into a democratic workplace.

We cannot be surprised when people seek more power over their lives by trying to get "their way". It helps if people can put this energy to creative use. If they can't, there may be power struggles.

To work well together, collective members must share goals and ideals. If this isn't the case, conflict can arise over almost any topic.

There are dozens of tough issues that can cause conflict. Conflict will be part of any group. It is a necessary and creative part of every relationship. Conflict should be treated as something natural, even useful. It challenges all of us to change and grow. When conflict becomes destructive and causes hurt feelings, it can lead to lasting problems, and can cause the break-up of a group.

Learning to resolve conflicts is one of the most important skills we can develop. Once we gain this skill, we can become strong and powerful in our abilities as social change agents.

### Ways of Dealing With Conflict

Avoidance. People ignore their feelings, look the other way, leave, go to sleep, or deny that there's a problem. Unless you plan to leave town, avoidance is not a very healthy way of dealing with conflict.

Smoothing things Over. This style delays the conflict. Some people may try to play up areas of agreement. They may resolve minor conflicts while avoiding the major ones. Another style is to keep issues so unclear that dealing with them is impossible.

Forceful Confrontation. This tactic at least addresses the conflict, but in a negative sense. Yelling, physical force, punishment, and sarcasm are all ways this method is used. It may seem to be effective for the "winner", but for the "loser", the real conflict may have just begun. She or he may be left feeling hurt or hostile as a result.

Compromising. This is often seen as a positive way of resolving conflict when people reach a solution they can live with. But compromise has a negative side. It may mean both sides lose, and neither gets what it really wants. Both sides try to resolve differences by settling for a second choice, or the lowest common denominator they can go along with. It's often an "easy way out", which doesn't really address the important issues.

Negotiating. Both sides can win with this method. It seems to have the potential of coming up with creative solutions which meet the most needs. Later in this chapter we'll describe a method for negotiating.

## Types of Conflict

There are at least three kinds of conflict. Try to figure out which kind you are involved in. The first is issue oriented. "I like Tony, but he never gets the books done on time." The second kind is personal. "Tony and I don't get along, and he never does the books on time." (Or just, "Tony and I don't get along.") People who are having problems getting along find more issues to disagree about. In this second case, people should work on improving their relationship before dealing with the issue of the books. The last kind is a values conflict. "I think keeping accurate books is an important part of running a business, and Tony thinks that's just a value of the capitalist system." These are often the hardest to resolve. Many times the best we can do is come to an understanding of what each other believes.

## Raising and Resolving Conflicts

Earlier in this chapter we mentioned some guidelines for giving feedback. Many of us find it easier to talk about the other person when we have a conflict. These are called "Messages". They begin with the word "you." "You always want attention," "You expect everyone to be perfect," "You leave the meeting room a mess! " But, if you tell someone how you feel about their behavior, you can turn your comments into "I-messages." The general "formula" is

"When you --- (unacceptable behavior), I feel --- (feeling word), because --- (consequences of their behavior)." The "you-messages" given above might look like this when translated into "I-message" form; "When you ask me questions a lot, I feel frustrated because I can't get my work done"; "When you criticize my writing, I feel hurt because I don't have a sense of what you liked about it"; "When you leave your papers and coffee cups on the meeting table, I feel angry, because I end up doing more than my share of cleaning." Of course it will feel unnatural to you to use this phrase at first. Try to be aware of how you tend to give criticism. "I-messages" seem to provoke less resistance, defensiveness, and struggle, making criticisms easier to hear.

It is important that people be active listeners. How do you know when someone is really listening to you? Try to answer this question and you will find some of the elements of active listening.

Usually someone is leaning in your direction, looking at you and sometimes nodding. They draw you out to say more, and they summarize what they've heard to make sure they're getting it. They allow time for you to express your feelings, and try to bring out your feelings. They don't let their own values and feelings get in the way of hearing what you want to get across. Sometimes they seem able to see the world from your point of view. When people are resolving a conflict, it's important for them to listen actively to each other before they start to respond to each other.

Six Point Problem Solving.

When people involved in the conflict sit down to discuss it, it helps to have some kind of process for resolving differences. Thomas Gordon, author of *Parent Effectiveness Training*, describes a six step process people can use.

Step 1: Identify and Define the Conflict

People should come to some agreement on what the problem is. We'll use an example of cigarette smoking at meetings as an issue. Each person should state their *needs* in relation to the problem. This is hard, because people tend to offer solutions as needs, and confuse the two. "I need clean, fresh air to breath, because I'm allergic to smoke" is the need; "I need people who smoke to leave the room" is the solution. "I need to smoke one cigarette an hour at least" is a need; "I need other people to let me do what I want" is a solution. List all the needs on paper where everyone can see them.

Step 2: Brainstorm all the Possible Solutions

Make a long list of every way you can think of to solve the

problem. The purpose of brainstorming is to get lots of ideas, to build on each other's ideas, to get as wild as you want, and to not judge or criticize any ideas. A list about the smoking problem might look like this;

- have smokers leave the room to smoke
- have nonsmokers leave the room when smokers want to smoke
- take a five-to-ten minute break every half-hour
- don't allow smoking
- have smokers stay at one end of the room near a window
- allow each smoker one cigarette an hour
- only have one person smoking at a time
- have smokers chew tobacco instead

Step 3: Eliminate Unacceptable Solutions

Is there anything on the list someone couldn't live with? If so, cross it out. If all the solutions get crossed out, go back to Step 2 and find some more ideas. Usually there are a few left that seem acceptable to everyone.

Step 4: Find the Best Acceptable Solution

Of the solutions left, which meets the most needs from the list made in step one? Is there a way to combine the solutions? In the example of smoking, the group may decide to have smokers near the window, only have one cigarette at a time, and to take a break if a nonsmoker feels the air is getting too thick. Write down the solution and make sure everyone agrees to it.

Step 5: Plan to Put the Solution into Action

Here is where you figure out the who, what, when, where, and how of putting your solution into practice. When does this policy take effect? How long will we try this for? Who should enforce it? How will we let people know who weren't here? Write down responsibilities taken.

Step 6: Follow-up and Evaluation

Plan a time to meet again to check in on how the solution is working. You may have to modify your original decision.

Although the example used was for a group problem, this process can also work for a conflict between two people. You may have to allow people a chance to vent their feelings before getting down to the business parts of the problem solving. Also, it helps to end this process by saying some things you like about each other. That helps you remember that you do care about the people you work with, and there is more to your relationship than struggling.

## Issues of Affection, Rejection, and Sexuality

There is not a collective where these issues have not affected the work of the group. If there is not honesty about sexual tensions, the collective can be badly damaged. Often, the worst damage occurs when secrets are kept about relationships that are starting, ending, or going through problems. The work relationships will be affected by this. While it is important to respect privacy, it is not really private when it affects the whole group. Even friendships may need to be dealt with, since they can also affect the group. Competition for someone's approval and friendship can cause tension.

Sometimes collectives that work with people find that some staff provide much better and more personal service to people of their sexually preferred sex. This can interfere with the work of the collective. People of the unpreferred sex may be badly served, and other members of the collective can become resentful. Because people can be defensive about their sexual behavior, these patterns might be hard to change.

## Good Feelings

Although it doesn't seem likely, problems can arise in a group in which people like each other too much. Research has shown that groups that are close tend to produce more. However, people still need to give honest feedback and criticism when they feel it. People cannot allow closeness to cause them to avoid problems that affect their work. Otherwise, the collective will suffer, and eventually the friendships will suffer, too.

## Social Issues

Sometimes it's hard to bring up problems that are not supposed to exist in collectives. This is particularly the case with classism, racism, sexism, and so on. However, collectives should be committed to working on oppression in the workplace. It means looking at how staff people relate to each other, and to the people they serve. Instead of denying our oppressive behaviors, we need to learn about them. As hard as it is to deal with these issues, working through them is very powerful, liberating, and rewarding.

## Burning Out

The turnover in collectives is rather high. Although there are lots of legitimate reasons why people leave, many people leave collectives because they are just plain burned out. They may not do any active social change work for several years. Operating a work collective should not have to mean being paid next to nothing for long hours with few benefits, but it often does. Low wages, and no paid sick time or health benefits are common in too many collectives. The time has come to realize that excessively low-paid overworked activists are no good to anyone.

Guilt-tripping is another factor in the burnout syndrome. There seems to be a social activists' version of the Puritan work ethic. While many of us involved in social change work claim we feel overworked, we reinforce that tendency in others. Several negative results occur. We define our importance in life solely through the political work we do. This limits our ability to work with people who don't define their importance that way, and limits the way people see social activists (i.e. always serious and always talking politics). We end up with the opposite effect of what we want. People are less apt to be attracted to the left.

A second negative effect occurs when we overextend ourselves. We may be into a lot of good stuff, but because we do so much, we are probably not doing our work as carefully or as well as it should be done. We end up forgetting a lot, missing deadlines, and being late for appointments.

Another related effect is that we turn off potentially active people. People who are not involved in social change get a sense from active people that their involvement has to be total. Otherwise they will continually feel guilty for not doing more. This has caused a tremendous loss of talent and energy in the social change movement. Collectives are only one place where this pattern occurs. We need to pace our energy better for the long haul. We need to accept and warmly welcome people's limited participation in social activism. None of us is so important that we need to keep our finger in every pie that interests us, as well as a few that don't.

There are other frustrations that occur in collectives and social action groups which could lead to burnout. One is a conflict between one's desire for personal growth, and the needs of the group. If this one keeps coming up, it may be a sign that someone should leave. And, there will be conflicts between the collective and the larger society. These conflicts can result in funding problems, lack of community support, or licensing difficulties.

To some extent, these problems cannot be avoided. Collectives need to limit what they expect to accomplish. They need to define clear and realistic goals, as well as ways to reach their goals. And, collectives need to provide ways for members to get lots of support.

Collectives work best when members share political visions and personal goals. They work best of all when people share an understanding of the relationship between social change, their own work, and the ways they want to grow and change as people.

The commitment to working out personal and group tensions brings together politics and personal styles. This commitment can make the difference between an ineffective collective and a powerfully dynamic one. But, if dealing with feelings becomes the main goal of the collective, then the group will become ingrown and deadening. Growth comes from meeting your environment and trying to effect change. Navel gazing is not growth. People need to place their sensitivity in perspective and balance it with the needs of collective work. The goal is to make feedback a means to the end of a collective's work, and not the end in itself.

# 7. Hirings, Firings, Leavings, and Salaries

Hiring, firing and salaries are some of the most sensitive issues in any workplace. They provide clues about the real organization of any group. They usually are decided very differently in a collective than in a traditional workplace. Hiring is often a shared process, firings are very painful, and salaries are not set on the basis of academic degrees or work experience. But, there are limits to how "alternative" these processes can be.

No matter how you do it, the reality of hiring is that the collective has power over the candidates. It would be ideal if a collective never had to fire someone. But there are jobs to do, payrolls to meet, and a society to change. Staff people who don't contribute can only be tolerated for so long. Concerning salary issues, collectives are often caught between wanting to provide decent level incomes, and wanting to spread their small financial resources as far as possible.

There are some things to keep in mind which help produce fairer and more human decisions about people. Decisions affecting someone in the collective have to be talked through fully with that person. There can be no backroom decisions. The needs of each person affected by or involved in any decisions must be heard and taken into account. These needs must be balanced against the needs of the collective as a group. We will offer you some guidelines and choices in dealing with these important topics. You can use them as a starting point for discussion.

## The Hiring Process

Given the informal way many collectives start, the first hiring decisions are often informal, too. People are added because they're available, because the small founding group likes them, or because they have useful skills and ideas. VSC, for instance, started with a core of three and added the next four in this way. As a group becomes more established, it moves towards more structure. Selecting from among friends means you are more likely to share visions and styles. However, this may mean you don't get people from a variety of backgrounds in your group. Opening up the selection process may help your group represent a wider community.

### Who Does the Hiring

When a collective wants to add or replace someone, the hiring process must be planned in advance. The method will depend on the situation. Collectives that work closely with lots of people will often hire from that pool of people. One Boston collective had a member's council. They invited energetic and unemployed people from that council to join the workforce and receive a salary.

Some collectives have personnel committees that design and run the hiring process. Others set up a different committee each time there is a vacancy. Yet others allow individuals to organize the process. A good rule in hiring is to start the process slowly and carefully. Once applications come in, in fairness to the applicants, you should make decisions fairly quickly. Once you are close to a final decision, you need to take time to be sure the decision is a good one.

In hiring, many collectives find it useful to involve outside people who are familiar with the needs of the collective. They can be helpful in making hard choices. They are not personally invested in the decision and can help point out issues as they arise.

### The Job Description

Once you decide the hiring method, a timeline should be drawn up, and decisions made about who will be responsible for what. There are some time-consuming but necessary chores involved, such as typing applications, getting ads out, writing and sending "rejection letters" and collecting resumes and applications.

The first major task is writing a job description, and deciding what qualities you want in the new staff person. This should be checked with the whole collective. Some things to consider are:

- Do you want to balance out the collective, in terms of race, age, sex, education or class background?
- What skill is the collective needing to add or replace?

• What ongoing work will the new person do, and what past experiences would be helpful?

• What are the personal expectations each staff member has of the new person? (It is very important to get these feelings out on the table early as they can cause problems later.)

• What view of social change and political action does the collective member need?

• What seems to make someone "work out" as a member of this group?

These questions could result in a huge job description. Try to keep it short and reasonable. At VSC, we have seen job descriptions that people couldn't fill. You can keep finer points in mind during the interview process. You also need to consider what special qualities someone needs to work in a collective setting.

Often groups want a minimum time commitment from someone, like one year or two. You should honestly say how hard someone is expected to work. Full time can mean fifty hours a week in some places. You should say this at the start, or it could lead to resentment later on.

### Spreading the Word

If you are going to hire someone you don't already know, the next step is to think about an advertising process. Some groups choose to spread the word through personal friends and other collectives. Others advertise widely. You should contact places where you'll reach the kind of people you're looking for. Mailings of notices to local groups, and ads in community papers and newsletters seem the best sources. If there are employment resource centers like VSC, jobs can be listed there. If there is a local *People's Yellow Pages* it can give you lots of good contacts. If you are part of a larger institution such as a university, there may be hiring guidelines you must follow.

### Applications

Now you need to consider some other questions. Will applicants be screened on the phone? Will everyone who fills out an application be interviewed? If not, how will applications be screened? How long will you accept applications?

To be fair, we think the process should move as quickly as possible. Tell people they are out of the running as soon as that decision is made. Too many workplaces take months to make hiring decisions. Remember, your applicants may be unemployed and need to find work soon. Respect them with an efficient hiring process. If your process is too long, you may also lose your best candidates.

What will you include on the applications? Is a resume enough? At VSC we tended to ask general questions about past work experiences and future goals for social change work. Other groups might focus on specific skills, or on interpersonal skills. You will be working very closely with this person, so talking about personal issues can be important.

Many collectives give out a packet of information with the application. This can include a job description, a description of the collective and its work, and an application form.

### Interviewing

In general, it is useful to have collective members talk out all their feelings *before* the final interviewing process. Some people may feel ripped-off by past hiring decisions. Others may have strong ideas about what they want from a new person. Some may have fears about particular kinds of people. You should reach some consensus about what you really want. This helps to avoid conflicts later.

The interviews themselves are crucial. There are several ways to arrange them. A health center interviewed a large number of people for a job as a health care worker. They set up a rolling interview. Candidates met with one small group to get to know the health center and discuss job commitments. Then they met with a second group to share what they would bring to the collective and what they would like to learn. The third group discussed the politics of health care. People who took part found this process useful. The group also gave them a sheet of the topics they wanted covered in the interviews, which did away with much of the need for formal questions. The decision-making process took several days.

VSC did a hiring by having candidates go through one interview with half the collective. Then the best qualified candidates were interviewed again by the whole collective, and some members of an advisory board. An all-day meeting led to the final choice.

At a law collective, lawyer candidates went through a two hour interview with eight people. It took two weeks to interview everyone, and at least six hours to reach a decision.

When interviewing, it is important to put people at ease as much as possible. You can show you value people for who they are. But making false promises or denying the fact that choices must be made is unfair. As mentioned earlier, power is in the hands of the collective. Decide in advance what questions you want to ask. If you have doubts about someone's politics, style or skills, it helps to raise those in the interview. This is hard to do, but it gives the candidate a chance to respond to your doubts.

Coming to a Decision

This is the hardest part of hiring. Ideally, if everyone was using the same criteria from the start, it would be clear which person to hire. It usually doesn't work that way.

People should not be pressured into accepting someone with whom they aren't comfortable. But, people must be honest about their doubts, and be willing to examine them closely. Once at VSC, a staff member was unhappy about hiring someone whose skills were only partly developed. The collective agreed to hire that person, provided everyone saw the problem and would work on it. Despite that commitment, a good program was not developed, and the new person only stayed a year.

In reaching a decision, you can go around the group and have people state feelings about the candidates. This may help narrow the field. Another way is for people to state and justify choices. Doing this might force people into opposing camps. Reaching consensus can then be hard. A VSC staff member once pushed very hard for one candidate. The rest of the group felt it had no choice but to block this. Only when the staff person backed off was that person hired.

At a law collective hiring, each staff person named his or her top three choices. Certain people's names kept coming up, which narrowed down the list of possibilities.

VSC has had noncollective people involved in the final interviews and in the hiring decision. We have found this to be extremely helpful. Collective members feel less fearful of being guilt-tripped into accepting someone they don't want. An outsider can push insiders to look at why they don't want a particular candidate. Such pushing by an insider could make matters worse.

Final decisions are hard. As with other consensus decisions, people can drop their favorite choice if they find other people don't accept that candidate. The best person may be different from the person with whom everyone is most comfortable. If people seem comfortable with the chosen candidate and look forward to working with her or him, that's good. If not, you are headed for trouble.

The pressures of this process can be intense. Sometimes people lose touch with their feelings. They agree to hire someone because it seems "politically correct." Or, people settle for the lowest common denominator. If you get stuck or tired, don't forget it's better to put off the choice than to make a poor one, but keep the candidates informed.

Above all, we encourage people to be gentle, and not to put unfair pressure on each other. A collective should support people in taking risks and making hard decisions.

Trial Periods

Some collectives have "trial periods" when they hire someone. VSC did not have good experiences with this practice. In one case, a person was vetoed after their trial time. After much pressure, this person was allowed in. It took years to heal the scars of suspicion and guilt. In other cases the trial period was a token effort. No real evaluation of the new person took place. If you ask people to work for a trial period they should be paid, otherwise there may be resentments.

It seems to us that these trial periods can work only if they are viewed as mutual. This means the new person also uses this chance to decide if she or he really wants to work for you. You should decide in advance why someone would be turned down. In general, we do not recommend "trial periods."

Many collectives use volunteers. VSC has and so have most groups. If you have a job opening, this can create tension among interested volunteers. Whenever VSC has had job openings, volunteers have usually applied. We have tried to deal with this issue openly and fairly, by having discussions with each of the volunteers who applied. But this is never easy. We have no suggested easy solution to this problem. But if you use volunteers and want open hiring for a job, be aware of this problem.

## The Firing Process

This may be the hardest issue in collectives. How can a work group that is committed to working on problems "ease out" a member? How does having loving concern for all members fit in with telling someone their time to leave the group has come? It does happen, and it has to happen. It may leave scars with the person involved and the group. But so can avoiding hard choices.

Collectives are committed to working together as a group. There is deep respect for the emotional and personal needs of all members. People are urged to be open about their weaknesses and to ask for support in dealing with them. That kind of trust exists only if people know their honesty won't be used against them. Therefore, collectives make pretty strong commitments not to fire people unless the problems are great. But workers have to be concerned with the services and work of the collective as well as treating each other with consideration. Members may come to feel a person is not pulling their weight, and the work of the group is suffering beyond repair.

Ideally, tensions between one worker and the rest of the collective are handled in meetings long before the issue of firing comes up. And it's hoped people who aren't working out will see the problem, and leave on their own. But, the personal closeness of collectives can make it hard to think and talk about these tensions. More often, things drag on. People feel more and more burned, until finally someone leaves, with a lot of pain. This pattern can be destructive. In a collective, the fired person cannot blame the system. Not to be wanted by people we respect is very, very hard.

### Problem Areas

There seem to be two main reasons people end up being fired. Usually they are related. The first is the ability to do the work. Sometimes collectives take on people who don't have the skills they need. Ideally some program is set up to train people properly. But, sometimes it just doesn't work out.

The other issue is personal relations. Some people attracted to alternative workplaces have been deeply hurt in other work settings. We have all been hurt by past experiences that can make us hard to work with at times.

### The Dynamics of Breakdown

There are many examples of these patterns. There are people who turn everything into a power struggle. Others insist that no decision can be made without an endless discussion of every aspect of the issue. There are those who come in late all the time, and those who feel their personal needs come before the collective's needs. Some people can't trust any subgroup of which they're not a part to make a decision; it's hard for them to give up responsibility to other people.

Sometimes these patterns can be worked on in the group, before things get too bad. Other times, distance between people gets so great, that the breaking point is reached.

Unfortunately, that breaking point is often handled badly in collectives. The person who is not "working out" may start to feel more and more hurt and excluded. They may turn up for work less and less. Or that person may stay around all the time and become progressively more hostile. At the same time, the people in the collective become more and more hostile and unwelcoming to the person who does not fit into their world. They start to exclude her or him even more.

Finally, according to this pattern, somebody lays down an ultimatum – "either you go or I do." Sometimes the ultimatum is clear and explicit, more often hidden and implicit. Once a decision is made, it may be easier to have an honest discussion of what happened. VSC has had some excellent "goodbye sessions" in which the pain was put on the table and dealt with.

## Towards an Honest Process

Clearly the pattern described above is a bad one. We felt, however, that this negative pattern should be honestly described, since it has been seen in collective after collective. We don't think people should blame themselves if it happens in their group. And, we don't want people to be discouraged about the collective model because of the difficulty of the issue. But, we do think it's important to try to find better ways of dealing with it. We hope that collectives will experiment with better ways of handling such problems, and will communicate the results to each other.

One collectively run co-op had a procedure for firing someone that involved the suspension of consensus. If 60 percent of the workers felt that someone had to go, they could get that person fired with the approval of the members' council. There was a one week cooling off period in which the person had the chance to change his or her behavior and be given a second chance. Both the firing statement and worker's response were in writing. This firing technique was used in the case of someone who people found "interpersonally impossible." We would recommend a longer period during which attempts could be made to work things out, and to provide time for outside input and help in resolving the problems.

There are several points about any fair firing process. The process should be very specific, and allow flexibility. Anyone asked to leave a collective should know the exact reasons for the request. The person in question should have a chance to change her or his behavior, or to gain the necessary skills to do well in the collective. Outside people respected by all parties can be involved in trying to work things out.

Paul Bernstein and Lew Bowers see firing as a last choice, they suggest several options to try before resorting to firing.[1] Let's say that you are having problems relating to Tony at work; he is constantly late to meetings, doesn't seem to be as committed to work as he once was, and reacts defensively to any sort of criticism or questions concerning his behavior.

The first step would be to talk to him about how you see his behavior affecting the collective. This includes the day-to-day operations as well as the overall goals and purposes of the group.

If that doesn't seem to have an effect, and others in the group noticed the same problems, several of you could approach him. Perhaps hearing it from more people would have more impact. He may need to hear information on what he does well, as well as where he falls short. He may need suggestions on specific ways he could resolve the shortcomings (like coming on time, being open to feedback, and so on).

If he can't take in the information you're giving him, there are probably some feelings that need to be expressed. He needs a safe opportunity to express any resentments and fears he has that are under the surface. Sometimes just expressing those feelings can clear up a problem.

However, sometimes that isn't enough. There may be deeper blocks that will require more time and effort to get to. At this point, you can change his job to focus on his strong points, but avoid giving him other responsibilities that he doesn't do well. You may also want to suggest some places he might go for more experienced help in changing, such as some kind of counseling.

A leave of absence might be the right thing to do at this point. It gives the person time to think, gives the collective a chance to calm down, and gives Tony a second chance with the group when he returns.

If all this fails, it is probably time to fire him. Keep in mind that you are not rejecting him as a human being, but just making the statement that "we cannot work well together."

Such ideas are easier to put on paper than to live in practice, but they are important. We suggest collectives talk about this subject before it is an issue. You can then decide what kind of process you would like to use. An important note: sometimes pushing everything into the light of day can be even more destructive to the person who is leaving. That person should have the option to discuss openly the issues, and should not be forced into it. If the worker wants to leave quietly, the collective should accept this. In such cases, the remaining collective can still learn much from discussing the issue thoroughly and carefully. The pain and guilt are never only on one side.

Firings are very hard. When collectives really know how to handle them, it will be proof that our movement has reached a high degree of maturity.

**Leavings**

People put a lot of emotional energy into collective work. Often they find it very hard even to consider moving on to other work. But, often an individual's personal development will take them out of the collective. People have left VSC to start a day care center, enter law school, become a professional musician, and do workplace organizing. If someone is feeling limited by the work of the collective, or if they just want to experiment with new things, it makes sense for them to move on. At the Bicycle Repair Collective, several people realized that their day-to-day repair work was keeping them from effective involvement in the social change movement. They left, but slowly, so that the collective was able to plan for and survive the leavings.

Often the idea that someone might leave the collective is threatening. Sometimes other members share similar doubts about their work, or may fear for the future of the collective. A healthy supportive collective gives people the space to think through how they want to plan their own lives. While we clearly value our coworkers, we must give them the space to see and meet their own needs, even if it means they move on.

One way of doing this is to provide time for people to talk about their future plans. Another is to encourage people to do the kinds of work they enjoy in the collective. This helps people get in touch with what they want to do. Perhaps collectives can be flexible about allowing members to work part-time as they set up their own projects. Collectives should pay unemployment insurance so that when collectives lay off people, they can collect unemployment.

At their best, collectives provide a supportive environment

where people can learn skills and gain confidence. People can do things they would never have believed themselves capable of before. Some people take their collective experience and use it in their new work.

Of course, leavings are not always planned and pleasant. Even when they are, both the person leaving and the remaining collective can learn a lot by talking about how everyone feels about the collective. Everyone should get a chance to express their sense of loss, grief, or relief when someone leaves. Keep in mind that anytime someone is added to, or leaves a collective, the whole group will be affected.

## Salaries

There are a number of ways to pay people in collectives, each with its own philosophy. Your salary system can reflect your goals and ideals. Many people don't work in collectives because of the money. In general, collectives should balance decent pay with doing as much work as possible.

### How much?

The issue of salaries and money in general brings up a lot of feelings. Some people think collective workers should be paid as much as those in similar traditional jobs. They argue that they work hard and have to survive in a society in which people's basic needs are met mostly with money. They think collectives aren't effective models of social change if they exploit workers.

Others take a different position. They point out that people who work in collectives get the enormous advantage of controlling their work lives. Therefore, they should be willing to sacrifice some money. They also point out that there are simple ways of living cheaply in many cities. Some believe that salaries should be low, so people don't participate in taxes, militarism, and consumerism.

This debate could go on forever. People need to understand the roots of their position, and stay flexible about this issue. However, often there is no alternative to low pay. If people want higher pay, they may have to move on.

### Different Models of Pay

Some of the more traditional ways of paying people are by seniority, by productivity, by how many jobs a worker can do, or by how "professional" a worker's skills are. Collectives are moving away from these types of differentiations between people. There are at least two methods with which collectives are experimenting.

One is to pay everyone in the collective at the same salary, regardless of what work they do. This is very easy to put into practice. It seems to support the democratic philosophy many collectives have. In this system, everyone's work is valued equally, from typing or administrating to selling or cleaning up. It can allow people to work different numbers of hours if they want to. This system seems easier to use with concrete services, like repair work. It can create problems if people with more skills feel a need for some recognition.

The other option is to pay in relation to what people need to live in a comfortable, simple lifestyle. The obvious catch here is that it's very tricky to define *need*. You must have a close group in order to work this out, and you will have to put a certain amount of time into talking through interpersonal issues.

A third alternative combines aspects of the methods described above. People are paid the same, but people with children are paid more. For example, Red Sun Press (Boston) has three collective members with children. They are paid $1 per hour more for each child.

Money is a hard issue. We encourage people to think carefully through what they need, and how it fits into the overall political structure of the collective. Some useful ways of looking at salaries might include the following questions:

- How much do I really need to survive?
- How much do I need to feel secure without help from outside?
- What would a different salary structure mean for the collective and its program?
- What are the real reasons for my needs? Are there other ways of meeting those needs?
- How will I feel about this salary structure after a year?

Setting salaries is just another issue where collectives are forging through new territory. There aren't many role models for alternatives to the traditional way of looking at salaries. You may become frustrated at times, but keep in mind that you are a part of a very complicated issue. Whatever you do and learn now will help collectives in the future.

## NOTES

1. Paul Bernstein and Lew Bowers, "Democratic Organization and Management," *Communities* (29) 1977: 26-39.

# 8. Special Problems of Collectives

As is true for small businesses in general, many collectives have started and folded in a few years or less. There are many possible reasons for this. Certainly one of the biggest problems collectives face is financing, such as lack of funding and lack of government support, etc. Addressing that issue is beyond the scope of this manual. (See Appendix Four for resources) But, research has shown that there are two other problems which keep cropping up in collective after collective. One is a lack of structure, and the other is a tendency towards too much structure. In this chapter we'll look at how both occur, and how they can be dealt with.

**Structurelessness**

In Chapter One, we discussed how the current growth of collectives started in the sixties, partly as a reaction against traditional ways of living and working. People had bad feelings about bureaucracy, hierarchy, and "the system." Some people based their new groups on a model of "the opposite of anything that exists must be better." An example is the free school movement. Teachers worked on an antitheory that was based on simple opposition to the mainstream: "They ring a bell, so we won't ring a bell; they take attendance, so we won't take attendance." Since much of our society seemed based on overstructuring, people became suspicious of all structure. There was an idea that if we just got rid of all the old restrictions, cooperation would develop naturally. As many groups have painfully found out, it just doesn't work that way.

In 1972, Jo Freeman wrote an informative article on the "Tyranny of Structurelessness" that is still relevant today.[1] She suggests that we must lose our prejudices about organization and structure. There is nothing basically bad about either. They can and are misused, but that isn't a reason to reject them. We need them as tools for growth.

### Why Structurelessness Doesn't Work

In reality, there is no such thing as a structureless group. Every group of people will structure itself somehow. It may not be planned or formal, but there is a structure. When it isn't out in the open, only a few people make or know the rules. They end up with more power. So really, we can't decide whether to have a structured or structureless collective – only whether or not to have a formally structured one.

When there is no structure, it often ends up that a small group of people, usually friends, informally take power in the whole group. They relate to each other more than to other people. They listen better to each other and interrupt each other less. They repeat each others' ideas and compromise easily.

These people didn't sit down and plan to take over. They are just friends who happen to be working together. Who gets to be in this group? Usually there is an unspoken set of standards (e.g. being middle class, being married, not being married, being gay, being "hip" or radical, having children, not having children). This group will push to hire new people who "fit in." Freeman says it is often like a sorority pledging new members.

There are two negative outcomes of this system. One is the informal way decisions get made. People will listen to others because they like them, not because they say important things. Also, this informal group has no responsibility to the group at large. Members will take the others in whatever direction they want.

A member of a health center told this story.

> I finally just had to leave and it was painful. The problem was that I spent a whole year setting up the center without working closely with anyone. There was no collective. Once the center was set up some people assumed I was the director, even though the word was never used and other people resented my power. Since I had been involved for so long I knew exactly what I wanted and what was best and anything anybody else did that was bad just reinforced my attitude, that I knew what was best. People who wanted it to be a collective would try at

> first to change things, and they would get frustrated and leave. That only left people who were perfectly willing for the center to be run hierarchically, which was not at all what I wanted. But there I was, not only in it, but heading the damn thing. I had to leave. It was the only way to get out of the box I'd put myself in. If I had it to do over again, I'd first find three or four people that trusted and respected each other and shared a political perspective before setting up a center.

Another resulting problem of structurelessness is the "star system." This has a tendency to occur in public groups such as organizing groups. The public and sometimes the media look for spokespeople. If no one is put forth by the group, someone will be put in that role by default. Sometimes it will be the person who has been there the longest, the oldest person, or someone who has drawn media attention for some event. It is hard to remove people from this role, and sometimes resentment can build up towards them. One way to deal with this is to assign one or two people to be spokespeople at an event. At the next event or demonstration you can pick different spokespeople.

Unstructured groups aren't very good for getting things done. People tire of "just talking," spending lots of time in meetings, or seeing exciting projects start and die out.

In the extreme, if people don't accomplish much work, they turn their energies to controlling others in the group. This isn't done so much out of a desire to hurt others, but a lack of anything better to do with their talents. When there is no clear structure there is usually lots of criticism, infighting, and personal power games.

Collectives must set up a clearly understood structure. Otherwise an unclear one will emerge and eventually destroy the group.

### How to Avoid Structurelessness

We are free to design forms of organization best suited to healthy collectives. This means we don't have to imitate traditional workplaces to survive. Collectives have to experiment, and develop different techniques for different situations. In this manual we try to present different methods to choose from, in setting up decision making, dividing up jobs and setting salaries.

In her article, Freeman suggests we keep in mind the following ideas on democratic structuring.

- Give specific jobs to specific people; don't let it happen by default.

- Require people to be responsible to the larger group.
- Distribute authority among as many people as possible.
- Rotate tasks among people.
- Give tasks to people for rational reasons. Ability, interest and responsibility are good reasons – being liked is not a reason for someone to get a job.
- People should have equal information whenever possible.
- Share resources and skills in the group.

**Overstructuring or "Bureaucratization"**

Structurelessness tends to be a problem in the earlier history of a collective. Collectives tend to become more and more structured as time goes on. Soon they may begin to look like traditional workplaces. There are lots of ideas about why this happens.

The basic values taught by our parents and the culture have a strong influence in our lives. The old scripts in the back of our minds about how a workplace should run get revived. People may want clear lines of authority to make it easier for everyone to know who is responsible for making and carrying out decisions. Hierarchies start to form.

As we get older, we may become more concerned with career advancement and good salaries than with political ideals. Many times people who have been in a collective for a long time are looked at in a strange manner by their friends. The idea that someone would want to work in a collective throughout their lives or for longer than five years is seen as strange. The subtle message is that collectives are fine when you're in your twenties, but that you should move into a professional better-paying job (which is what your friends have probably done) as you get older. Sometimes this attitude is based on people's hopelessness about making real changes in society through collectives. Many collective "veterans" in Boston have felt this pressure. It can lead to a more conservative structure for the group in order for people to become professional and make higher salaries. The structure becomes rigid. The goal of the group becomes keeping itself going as ideals begin to fall by the wayside.

How it Happens

Gordon Holleb and Walter Abrams have studied several agencies in depth.[2] They have seen a set of stages collectives go through over time – usually within a few years.

The first stage is when the collective is full of high energy, confusion, lots of ideals, and small groups of friends. In time, it becomes clear that some members are more competent, responsible, and committed than others. Those people push for less of a focus on ideals and more of a focus on delivery of services.

After that, there may be power conflicts between the core group and other staff. To deal with this, certain people gain more power. This leads to a crisis point in the group. The staff realizes that little by little, it has lost the values it started with. At that point, the group has two choices.

The staff members can shrug their shoulders, sigh regretfully, and move on to a more bureaucratic and hierarchical structure. Boston's *Real Paper* was an example of this first choice. At one time it was a worker controlled and owned paper. The workers, in the name of efficiency, began giving more power to fewer people. In a short time, a full scale hierarchy developed. There were high salaries for some, bonus pay scales, and individuals who could hire and fire people. Some workers left who disagreed with what was going on. Finally, the *Real Paper* was sold to a group which included David Rockefeller, Jr.

The other choice for the group is a compromise. Members try to meet some of the obvious problems while developing an improved collective structure. We hope this manual will help with those efforts.

The two problems discussed in this chapter will continue to diminish as we learn from each other's experiences. No one said collective work would be easy. Social change requires a lifelong commitment to the belief that there is a better way of running things. When we give up on that commitment we are accepting the inevitibility of our oppressive society. We must give each other enormous support to continue to find more joyful ways of living and working.

Joyce Rothschild-Whitt has come up with some conditions that help groups to stay democratic in the way they function.[3] Some are related to the collective's internal dynamics, and some to how the collective relates to the outside world.

It is often better for a group to break up than to change its original goals. One free medical clinic closed rather than charge for services, even though money was a problem. A food co-op wrote in its bylaws that if a certain number of co-op members didn't show up for three general meetings in a row, the co-op would begin to dissolve.

Another suggestion is to keep wages and benefits fair, but low. Not so low as to risk losing good people, but not so high that you start encouraging people to protect their positions at any cost to the group. You should largely depend on the collective itself for financial and emotional support. That means outside grants are not desirable in the long run. They can only give financial stability on a year-to-year basis.

It helps if your group wants to put out some service or product that is not easily available or easily affordable from traditional business. Preventive health care, nutritional foods, and radical literature are examples of the things collectives offer which are hard to find. Legal assistance and health care are examples of things that are not affordable for many working people.

Getting support from progressive professionals in the area can be helpful. Doctors may donate time to a local free clinic. College professors may send students to work with you as volunteers. Many colleges have internship programs in which students can receive credit for working with you. The last two editions of the Boston *People's Yellow Pages* would never have been done without the energy and commitment of student interns. It's a good way for them to start to get a taste of social change work.

Finally, keep in touch with the broader movement for social change. You are part of "one struggle with many fronts."

## NOTES

1. Jo Freeman, "The Tyranny of Structurelessness." *Berkeley Journal of Sociology* (17) 1972-73: 151-64.
2. Gordon P. Holleb and Walter H. Abrams, *Alternatives in Community Mental Health* (Boston: Beacon Press, 1975).
3. Joyce Rothschild-Whitt, "Conditions for Democracy: Making Participatory Organizations Work," in *Coops, Communes and Collectives: Experiments in Social Change in the 1960s and 1970s* ed., John Case and Rosemary Taylor (New York: Pantheon Books, 1979).

# 9. Collectives and Social Change

Working collectively is a political and social statement in itself. The government and most workplaces, schools, families and churches are hierarchies. These structures tend to give power to a few people, and leave the rest powerless. The collective ideal sits in opposition to the general rule in our society. It calls for equal power in decision making, equal status, and equal or needs-based pay. People who form collectives are committed to positive human interactions and good work experiences.

If the group is interested in being part of a larger social change effort, creating a collective is not enough. We have seen too many collectives turn inward to meet only their own needs. Some become confused about their goals, and how their day-to-day processes relate to those goals. Others have basically come to be just like the institutions they initially sought to challenge. Many criticisms have been voiced about collectives by people in the social change movement.

How do collectives relate to the larger movement for social change? The answer lies partly in what kind of movement for social change we want to see. The movement involves a long process of revising work and community life. Its main goal is that all of us will gain control of our lives from the few who control and maintain the institutions now. It will require direct action by those who don't have that control.

In the meantime, the movement is carried on in many small ways. Besides work collectives, there are workplace organizing efforts, feminist activities, community organizing, tenant's action, women's and men's support groups, people's culture and media projects, and gay and lesbian liberation efforts. Instead of waiting till "after the revolution," many groups are showing how working and personal relationships can be improved right now.

## The Collective Experience

Collectives give people a chance to experience a healthier work process. Working in a collective involves both control and responsibility. We can do what we really care about doing, while learning that the effect of our work rests on us, and not on a boss. We also learn to balance the group's needs and the individual's needs.

The collective can be a model of how work can be liberating rather than always oppressive. Without models of better ways of working, we are stuck with the only things we know. This includes competition, hierarchy, classist, racist, sexist attitudes, and profit-oriented assumptions. When people who are committed to social change experiment with new forms of work, they provide models for new styles of relationships. This is a significant service to the movement.

## Limitations of Collectives

There are, however, some problems inherent in creating alternative institutions within a capitalist society. Paula Greise offers an excellent analysis in an article on food co-ops which appeared in a magazine called *North Country Anvil.*[1]

> Co-ops cannot be 'politically neutral,' for there is no such thing. Nor can they make a revolution – or any kind of significant change – merely by existing and growing. It is important to recognize the criticism made clear back in the 18th century by pre-Marx British 'Levelers': namely, it is not possible to build an alternative society quietly and peacefully, wholly 'outside' the mainstream society, for the latter's rules control most of the wealth and the means of producing new wealth (land, minerals, energy supplies, factories, tools). If an alternative looks likely to threaten this, they may fight it. If you cannot defend your 'alternative,' they win.
>
> Struggles for control must go on inside existing institutions, where most of the resources are located, and most of the people are working. People's co-ops can be small 'utopian' models, and survival centers for such struggles. But the food industry will not become 'people controlled' by the building of co-ops. Not while there exists the A&P (world's largest retail network),

> the United States Defense Department, Tenneco (oil, factory, farms conglomerate), Pillsbury, General Foods, Green Giant, Ralston Purina, International Minerals and Chemicals, IT&T, International Harvester, etc. Co-op people should ask themselves how they can best aid struggles within such power-controllers as these corporate giants. This may lead to more fruitful strategies which would achieve the Rochdale pioneers' purpose: Not a 'people's store,' but a 'people's world.'

History has shown that collectives and alternatives are not going to create an alternative society that will replace capitalism. Many people who worked on setting up collectives and co-ops in the 1960s thought that the very existence of these new structures would bring about the end of capitalism. This alone will not be the way.

**Collectives and Worker Control**

Some people see work collectives as the seed of worker control and a worker managed economy. People learn the skills of collective control, see it's positive effects, and recognize its usefulness. In another sense, collectives are not that seed. Large workplaces will only become collectively run through organizing. That effort is part of the current progressive trade union movement. To become completely collectivized, our economic system will have to change.

There have been efforts to bring worker management into larger workplaces in the United States. If started by management they often are attempts to pacify workers or increase production.

Sometimes workers will buy out a company that is threatening to leave the area, and manage it themselves. These efforts do make a contribution to the movement, but the company still must compete with capitalist companies in a capitalist market. This has been the downfall of many alternative workplaces.

There are books listed in Appendix Five where you can read more about efforts at collectivization in this and other countries.

**How Groups Oppress Each Other**

Oppression occurs when one group gets social and economic benefits at the expense of another, and cooperates in mistreating the other. In our society and in many others, young people, old people, people of color, women, working class people, gay, lesbian, and bisexual people, and disabled people are oppressed. People from different ethnic groups have also been oppressed at various points in history. Most of us are part of at least one oppressed group, and we are also part of some oppressor group. Oppressive attitudes are built into the media, religion, business, government, education and the legal system. This is called "institutionalized oppression."

Another important concept is "internalized oppression." This happens when people of a given group start believing all the negative things that are said about them. Historically two clear examples of this are what occured to Blacks in this country and Jewish people under Nazism. People have been taught, and are still being taught, that Blacks and Jews were passive during their oppression and annihilation. This is totally false and racist. Yet, because of this, Blacks and Jews are two of many groups that have suffered incredible damage from this "internalized oppression."

Most groups suffer from internalized oppression. Women may think they're not attractive unless they have a certain body build. Young people may think that their ideas are not valuable. Gays and lesbians may consider themselves "sick" and feel badly about their homosexuality. One result of this internalized oppression is that people in the same group can be hostile to each other. Young people may tease and criticize each other in a hurtful way. Women may not get close to each other, because they feel competitive over men.

We believe that oppression exists because it is a way to keep those in power from having to give up or share that power. Internalized oppression can make us accept a "victim" role, where we don't fight back against oppression. Oppressed groups get caught up in fighting each other, instead of working together.

Here are some important points to keep in mind about these issues:

- Guilt doesn't do anyone any good. Don't get stuck feeling horrible about all the things you've ever said or done that may have hurt someone else. It's not your fault that you were raised to do or think those things. You can use your energy to start changing right now.
- All groups of people can be prejudiced. But people of color are victims of racism from the power structure, women are victims of sexism, and so on. Blacks are not racist because they have no power (as a group) to implement racism against whites.
- Sometimes, members of a group may need to spend time together, separate from everyone else. They do this to get support, share stories, feel safe and get a better sense of who they are. This

can be very threatening for people who aren't in that group.

• It should not be left up to the members of a particular oppressed group to handle all of their own concerns. It's very important that we become "allies" of each other. Men can interrupt sexist comments by other men. White people can do racism trainings for other white people. The idea is "none of us is free until all of us are free."

To become allies, we need to become more aware of what the issues and problems are of each oppressed group, how we contribute to the oppression, and how they want us to become their allies. Until we work on our own oppressive attitudes, we won't be able to make the workplace safe for oppressed groups, as coworkers or clients. This is very hard and scary for most of us and we need lots of support.

Using oppressed peoples' attention and time to relieve our guilt or express our anger and fear is just another form of oppression. A final caution about this; oppressed people don't ever need to listen to oppressor people's "material." For example, it is important for heterosexuals to work on their heterosexism with each other, middle class people to work on their classism with other middle class people, and so on.

**Oppression in the Workplace**

In a collective, working on oppression is important. There are some aspects of working together where issues of oppression are important to consider.

One is the make-up of the staff. You want people from varied backgrounds, and people who can meet the needs of the community you want to serve. Accessibility is an issue. If you are in the country or the suburbs, and people need cars to get to you, you are excluding many young or working-class people from using your service. If people are expected to be at your place for a while (like picking up a food co-op order) and you don't have childcare facilities, you risk excluding single parents. If your store or office is inaccessible for wheelchairs, some disabled people will not reach you. What servcies you offer also reflects your sense of oppression issues. Should a food co-op not stock "junk food" even if it's what the community people want? Do the health care workers in a clinic know the questions to ask sexually active young people to get at their special concerns? Does the bookstore have a section on gay and lesbian literature? Keep these groups in mind.

## Women and Collectives

Women's collectives and feminists in collectives make up a large and exciting part of the collective movement. Women have the chance to regain control over an important part of their lives. They can rediscover their abilities and their values. Many collectives are committed to dealing with sexism, so that they become positive places to work. Even then, it's not easy. Other times, women choose to have a separate workplace or separate women's days within the schedule of a mixed collective. One reason they do this is to learn skills without always being seen as "one down." Work has been a male dominated aspect of society for a long time. Another reason some women choose to work in all women's groups is to develop new feminist approaches to problems.

Health is one area in which work has been done by women-only collectives. Women's health was once handled by women, but now it's dominated by men. Women are taking back that control, in self-help clinics, and natural childbirth or home groups. Women are coming to know about, heal, and care for their own bodies. This can be threatening to the male medical world.

Counseling is another service that women are offering to each other. For a long time, men have defined mental health. Women who didn't fill traditional roles were labeled "sick." Feminist therapists are changing that definition. They see that part of women's problems lie in the society itself, and not just in their heads. Feminist therapy collectives have helped all of us see that much of "our" problems are caused by society, and that we need to change society. Women counselors are also exposing the wide-spread problems of violence against women and children, a tragedy that has been ignored for too long.

Many women want to learn skills that only men usually learn. These include auto repair, printing, carpentry, and law. Such skills provide important survival tools in our society. Traditional work-places don't encourage women to learn these skills, and usually don't even offer any training programs. Women don't want to have to fight or be tough to get these skills and learn what they want. This is why some choose to work only with other women.

Dealing with childcare and work is a crucial issue for women (as well as to some men). Collectives can experiment with this issue. Some groups take on partial or total responsibility for childcare during work hours. Others include childcare costs in salaries. Sharing this responsibility frees up parents, and gives coworkers a chance to be with children. Any group that doesn't deal with this topic is limiting who can be on their staff.

Another issue is job roles. It's important that women not get stuck in certain job roles such as keeping the workplace clean, making coffee, talking about feelings, or doing secretarial work. Often, these traditionally "female skills" are not valued as much as "male skills." They are harder to measure and are taken for granted, even though they are crucial to any workplace. Everyone needs to see these skills as important, and this kind of work should be shared. Men need to think about giving women space to learn "male skills," such as running meetings, or being spokespeople to other groups and the media. Women who learn these skills can share them with each other.

### Class Issues

Working-class people make up a large sector of the powerless in our society. Collectives that offer legal help, health care and reasonably priced food are examples of services that are sorely needed by low income people. These collectives will have less trouble serving working-class people.

Other groups may offer their services in some way that is not attracting a variety of people. The service itself may not be something certain people would seek out, because it's not part of their daily life or culture. For instance, many food co-ops did not carry what they considered to be junk foods, like sweets, or foods with chemical additives. The more that co-ops were purists about the food they carried, the less they served the needs of many people. Most co-ops have changed this attitude. Instead of censoring the food the sell, they try to give helpful information about nutrition on signs in the co-op and in newsletters. And they still don't carry twinkies.

Another issue is location. Simply put, reaching low-income people requires that you be located in the neighborhoods where such people live and work.

Hiring is an important issue in working on classism. Often collectives will hire from their volunteer staff. Sometimes they will require people to go through a trial period. Both of these methods are unfair, because some people are not in a position to work for free. We suggest that collectives use more formal hiring processes and advertise jobs at places that are frequented by working-class people.

Having intellectual, abstract meetings full of long words or jargon can be a turn-off to people who aren't college educated. (They may also be a turn-off to college educated people.)

You may encounter some differences in how people from different class backgrounds view the issue of money. This can come up in salary decisions, charging for services, or what to do with profits. These differences need to be carefully discussed and worked out.

The changes and growth that come from people of different class backgrounds sharing and working together make working for social change more fulfilling and exciting.

### Race Issues

Although we're speaking in this section about people of color, we want to point out that each group (Black, Hispanic, Asian, Native American, etc.) has its own unique concerns, as well as some that are shared.

The collective movement has been mostly a White movement. White people need to take a hard look at why people of color haven't been attracted to collective work settings. Some issues will be raised here, but we encourage you to look for others in your workplace.

Most of us have been exposed to the practice of "tokenism." This takes place when a staff hires someone of a certain background to fill a requirement, to "look good" to the outside world, or to relieve guilt. It is not done because there is a sincere commitment to dealing with oppressive patterns. Collectives are not immune to "tokenism." Once hired, these people can experience some isolation, since their life experiences have been so different. One way to work against this is to make sure there is more than one person of color on the staff, whenever possible. They can support each other, and work together to challenge the racism they see among staff members.

Like other groups, people of color may choose to work only with each other, and form their own collectives. They may offer counseling services, cultural events, or other services which address basic needs like food, clothing, and shelter. Or, these collectives may organize around political issues affecting people of color all over the world.

If you are going to work with a multiracial staff, there are some other issues to keep in mind.

Remember that English is not everyone's first or only language. You may have to speak more slowly and clearly than usual at meetings to make sure everyone understands. Learning Spanish can be an important factor in reaching out to Hispanic people. Make sure any signs or literature you have around is translated into the languages of the people you serve.

People of other cultures may not be familiar with or comfortable with the orientation towards systems and structures that some collectives have, whether it be for running meetings, filling out forms, setting up appointments or dealing with feelings. Don't rigidly assume that everyone has to fit into "doing things your way"; find out what differences and feelings exist, and work out a mutually agreeable solution.

Many collectives choose not to carry products which require the exploitation of labor or resources in Third World countries. Some food co-ops have stopped selling bananas for this reason. Boycotting Nestle's products (because of their policy of selling harmful infant formula to mothers in Third World nations) is another example.

Sometimes groups hire a Third World person and put them in charge of that group's outreach efforts to people of color. This can work out well, but is not to be used as a substitute for *everyone* on the staff doing her or his best to examine her or his own subtle expressions of racism. In our way of thinking, racism is White people's problem and it shouldn't be left to people of color to handle.

This means that collectives should devote some attention to dealing with racism issues, whether or not they have Third World staff or clients.

## Gays and Lesbians in Collectives

One thing that is different about the oppression of gay and lesbian people as compared to that of other groups is that they are not physically different from other people. You can't tell if someone is gay or lesbian by looking at them.

The workplace is often the most oppressive area in a gay man or lesbian's life. They are often "in the closet" at work, even if they are "out" other places. It is often not safe for gays and lesbians to be open about their gayness. They open themselves up for hostile comments, rejection, loss of their jobs, and physical violence. There are many people who think homosexuality is sick, or find it very threatening. Even when applying for jobs, gay and lesbian people may not be able to put down their work with gay and lesbian groups on their resume. There is no way to be sure how someone will respond.

Sometimes gays and lesbians choose to work only with each other, because it's the only way they can feel safe to let go and be themselves.

Many gay and lesbian businesses that deal with cultural activities have opened up – bookstores, theater or dance groups, recording companies and music groups, magazines and publishing houses. They attempt to spread gay and lesbian culture that wouldn't be easily found in more traditional places. One outcome of the gay liberation movement is the discovery of the variety of gay men and lesbians who have contributed to our history and society.

Another growing field is counseling collectives for gays and lesbians. Like women who were unhappy in their traditional roles, homosexuals were labeled sick by the mental health profession. Every personal problem was seen as resulting from the fact that the person was not heterosexual. Therapy took the form of trying to "cure" them of their homosexuality. Now, gays and lesbians are helping each other deal with the special problems they encounter in an oppressive society.

One of the major ways gays and lesbians are oppressed is by services, languages and societies which assume that everyone is heterosexual. This can be very subtle. The collective should provide safety by making it clear that homosexuality is accepted and thought about. Don't assume that all women need birth control or have male lovers. Don't assume that everyone will have children, or assume that being gay or lesbian is just a matter of sexual preference. It is often a commitment to one's own sex – emotionally, politically, and spiritually. Being afraid of homosexuality is one of the things that keeps us from being closer to members of our own sex, and keeps us locked into limited sexual roles. Working on this "homophobia" will benefit all of us, not just gay and lesbian people.

### Issues of Age in Collectives

Most collectives seem to be made up of people in their twenties and early thirties. One way people are oppressed is because of their age. For different reasons, young people and old people are not valued in our society.

All of us were oppressed as young children. There were lots of things we didn't get to do, because the adults around us wouldn't let us. Sometimes this was based on sensible notions ("Don't touch the stove, or you'll get burned!") and sometimes not ("Stop crying and act like a big boy!"). As we get older we do the same thing to people younger than us.

Teenaged people have a very high unemployment rate. They aren't taught skills in school that they can "market," and most jobs are for people with lots of experience.

Older people also have a hard time finding work. People assume they're "too old to learn a new job," they "won't fit in," or "they will be too rigid." We also tend to believe that people lose their ability to think well as they get older. We automatically put down someone older for having a traditional lifestyle, which we see as unsuitable for "alternative" workplaces.

Many collectives are on somewhat shaky ground financially. This can make it hard for older people to work there, since they often have more financial obligations.

There are some ways to become more open to these two groups. If clients come in with their children, we shouldn't see and treat the children as a nuisance or a distraction. Keep in mind that they are just as human as we are. Ignoring them and ordering them around isn't what they need or deserve.

In Boston, collectives and social change groups have made use of a high school work-study program in which students are paid by the program to work twenty hours a week. The collectives that have used these programs and hired young people have high praise for the young people who work with them. And the young people involved have commented on how much more they have enjoyed the work. They felt respected and cared for by their older coworkers. They carry this valuable experience back to their schools and communities.

If you do hire young people, you should take their needs into account. In one collective of older people and teenage working-class people, the older people, who were mostly college educated, would dominate. The young people sat passively at meetings, even though they were leaders "on the streets." Finally, after their anger built up, the young people wrote a speech with the help of a thesaurus. They marched into the meeting, delivered it, and walked out. After that, the meetings became much better. If anyone did not understand what was being said, they spoke out immediately. The college educated older people were forced to learn to talk more clearly and concretely, and the young people learned meeting skills and a larger vocabulary.

Older people may also need support. They need to know you really are interested in what they have to offer. They can be valuable resources for your group. Some collectives have used the energy of retired people who have much to offer. A few years back, an older semiretired woman spent a year as part of the VSC collective. The experience was exciting and powerful for all of us. Needless to say, we also saw more older people coming to VSC.

One reality for many older people is that they may have some trouble seeing and hearing as well as they could at age twenty. Be conscious of this, make signs and charts big enough for everyone to see, and speak loud enough at meetings so no one has to strain to hear.

Sometimes collectives will offer a discount to senior citizens to draw in older people as customers. They need to know they are welcome in an "alternative store" full of young people. The Boston and Cambridge Food Co-ops do not require older people to work their required two hours per month in order to shop at the co-op. However, many active, retired people put in long volunteer hours and have set up programs to deliver cheaper co-op food to older and disabled people.

If you do hire an older person, be aware of how you may start treating them differently than other staff people. Most of us have unresolved issues and feelings towards our parents and other "authorities" in our lives who were usually older. Make sure you aren't laying those feelings on the older collective member.

### Challenging the Consumer-Profit Mentality

Capitalism has become more than a way of allocating resources in our society. It is a way of thinking. There seem to be two basic principles of profit-making capitalism. One is that businesses want people to buy as much as they can get them to buy. The other is that the business will charge as much as it can get for their service or product. Many collectives challenge this way of operating.

One difference is how collectives charge for goods and services. Some groups use a sliding-scale based on ability to pay. In some collectives, people pay what they earn in an hour for an hour of the staff's time. In Boston, several counseling collectives charge 10 percent of your weekly wages for a one hour session. (Remember, counselors cannot counsel forty hours a week). Other groups start with the basic budget needs and develop a scale that gives them enough money. Some cooperatives, such as food co-ops or childcare groups can charge less because members pay partly by working a few hours a month for the co-op. Occassionally, groups make arrangements for barter. This means they trade their services or goods for something other than money. Someone who knows carpentry could build mailboxes for the staff of a law collective, for example.

Another "challenge" is the way collectives handle their cash surplus. Some groups have decided to keep their salaries low. They donate their surplus to community groups. For example, Red Sun Press donates print work to needy social change groups when they have a surplus. It's important to let people know if you're doing this as most people assume that profit goes for expansion, higher salaries, or to investors.

One more way collectives question the consumer-profit mentality is through the self-help or teaching approach to service. Along with providing a service, the collective teaches people to do the work for themselves.

The Bicycle Repair Collective teaches people how to repair their bikes if they want to learn. People may also come in just to use tools. Rates differ depending on whether the collective members do the work, the customer does it with their help, or whether the customer just uses the tools. Similarly, self-help health centers teach women to do their own cervical and breast exams. By most business standards this is utter folly! It fosters self-sufficiency and means people are no longer at the mercy of the experts.

In rejecting the mentality of capitalism, collectives are developing what we might call a "serve the people" approach. The assumption behind this idea is not how much can we get you to buy and how much can we get you to pay for it. It's what we can do that will really be a service to you and how we can do it in a way that is most useful and empowering.

## Politics and Study Within the Collective

In order for your collective to have clear political direction, people need to have some agreement about political and social theory, goals and process. A certain amount of diversity is healthy. Some degree of conflict can be worked through in discussion and study. Whether or not there is a conflict, a discussion of social change and the nature of power in this society helps to keep everyone thinking and growing.

In collectives, we have a unique opportunity to talk about our ideas and questions within the context of our day-to-day work. However, it's sometimes useful to plan some work time for discussion and study. Some collectives have an organized study group or self-led class to talk about general issues of politics and economics. These often include readings. A good list of books and articles could be found through local political-education groups, resource centers, radical bookstores, women's centers, and even the local library. The Movement for a New Society has developed a study technique called the macroanalysis seminar which might be useful. The handbook has a detailed reading list on various topics. They are listed in Appendix Four.

Another model for discussion is one centering on specific political topics that relate to a collective's work. VSC has done some reading and discussing about workplace change and the pros and cons of unions. A health center has had weekly issue forums where they talked about politics and the politics of health care. Often our own ideas and experiences can be enough to discuss; other times readings help.

## Cooperative Relationships Between Collectives and Social Change Groups

Collectives need to work against isolation and competition by making connections between different kinds of social change efforts. There are lots of ways to do this.

There are magazines and newsletters by which groups doing similar kinds of work share what they're doing and learning. We provide a list of some of these in Appendix Four. There are also groups that sponsor workshops and conferences that are helpful to collectives. Appendix Four lists some of these groups.

More experienced people could be "loaned" to new groups which need help. People working in collectives become involved in other educational and organizing efforts. These collective workers bring their process skills to share, and in return they learn to serve better the needs of the people in their community.

Some collectives have offered loans to collectives that were starting up and needed some help. Other times, collectives have donated services or money to a worthwhile project of another collective. Such was the case with VSC's *People's Yellow Pages*, and both editions of this book. Offering workspace is another way groups can help each other.

There seem to be many areas in which collectives can offer support and ideas for change to people working in mainstream institutions. At the same time, they learn about some of the issues and realities of the traditional organizations.

In Washington, D.C., striking workers at a Safeway Supermarket linked up with workers at two collectively run foodstores. The collective members picketed Safeway, and Safeway workers handed out leaflets asking people to shop at the collectively run stores during the strike.

In 1972, there were three alternative magazines dealing with similar concerns – *Alternatives, Communitarian,* and *Communitas*. By December of that year, they merged their three into one publication, *Communities*. They have gone on to publish several books as well as a regular magazine.

Another example would be neighborhood groups joining together to form a cooperative day care center for the children in the area.

Another way collectives can work together is to use each other's services as much as possible. This serves to help keep our money and resources within our movement.

Earlier in this chapter we mentioned bartering as a way of exchanging goods and services. Collectives could use this system sometimes. Once a printshop was having some problems with its decision-making process, VSC traded counseling time for printing time.

Collectives tend to be busy keeping up with their own work and area of interest. It's hoped that they can make time to develop relationships with other groups. If all these different ways of connecting took place, we would have a stronger network of social change groups.

# 10. Closing the Circle: Collectives, the Movement, and Social Change

The collective movement has drawn heavily from the long history of the struggle for fundamental change in America. A new wave of collectives started at the end of the sixties when political activists realized that they needed to develop work forms that challenged hierarchy and depersonalization and that met their personal needs. To do this, they drew on their movement's experiments in SNCC and SDS with participatory democracy and flexible work structures. At the same time, many of these activists recognized that the New Left had at times abandoned its commitments to the equal worth of all people and allowed itself to become dominated by manipulative, usually male, leaders and "media heavies." The rebirth of the feminist movement, first in organizations like SDS and then in the larger society, was launched by radical women's insistence that the movement take seriously its own rhetoric about the equal worth of women. Similarly, the movement toward collective styles of work and organizing is based on a return to the egalitarian ideals of the New Left.

The collective movement is a potentially powerful part of a movement for social change, because it appeals to deeply felt ideals. People want to control their work and their lives. They want institutional structures that guarantee their right to this control. The collective movement provides a way for people to assume some of the control in their worklives.

People in collectives aim to spread their ideals throughout society. We want to show that worker ownership and control is not a pipedream, but a real possibility that has been blocked by those who will lose their power in a worker-controlled economy.

These ideas can be spread through political work and by taking collective ideals into traditional businesses and bureaucracies.

We know of welfare workers who have developed participatory work groups and fought for and won much greater freedom in the handling of cases, as well as improved conditions for recipients.

People who have had collective experience have helped organize community groups along collective lines. They have been involved in tenants' unions and groups fighting for urban "renewal." In some cases, they have won the right to decide what does and doesn't get built in their community.

Rank and file workers in union after union are forming democratically run caucuses and are working to return unions to the control of the workers. Workers are no longer satisfied with higher pay, but want control over their work as well. People who have worked in collectives have taken jobs in factories, mines and other large workplaces. They are using their experience in collectives to help build democratic rank and file movements. In unorganized workplaces, they are helping to organize workers to work for changes in the shop. And some collectives have become union shops. Red Sun Press joined District 65 (UAW) in order to be a union print shop, to take advantage of union benefits such as health insurance, and to support a progressive trade union.

We know people who have worked in collectives and then moved into state bureaucracies. They are trying to bring about shared responsibility for decisions within the hierarchy. People who have some status in a bureaucracy have given more power over to "subordinates." They encourage collective decision making and create flexible job roles. Occassionally, those at lower levels have been able to demand and get collective responsibility for running their programs. When turned down, they often form union organizing committees.

We don't believe that such pressures alone will build a worker-controlled economy. Real worker control is a fundamental change. It would be opposed by those who would lose in such a change.

In fact, this has happened in many cases already. Managers and directors start realizing the implications of workers' collectivity, and withdraw the reforms they put in. However, the important ideas have been spread. This is a vital first step in building the awareness in this country that workers can and should control the workplaces.

At its best the collective movement can respond to the deep

longings people feel for a better society. Collectives can demonstrate a long-term way of building a society based on the needs of the majority of the people. We can integrate those visions for a better society into our daily lives.

A movement for fundamental change in this country will only succeed if it offers a model of what we are working for, and a consistent way of working for it. This is the contribution of collectives.

# Appendix 1. Forms of Legal Organization

Every work group is organized in some way or another, either formally or informally. There are advantages and disadvantages to each form of legal organization. We'll explain each option in this appendix. Please keep in mind that this information isn't meant to substitute for a lawyer's help. First, there are exceptions to every rule in law. Also, each state has its own regulations, which you need to know. However, you can get a lot of background information in legal libraries and from government agencies.

If you get legal help, try to find a lawyer who is somewhat familiar with collectives or is in a collective. If you don't know of anyone, you can contact your local office of the National Lawyers Guild, and they can refer you to someone in your area. Once you find a lawyer, be clear about what work the lawyer will do and what the charge will be. Rates are usually determined on a "per hour" basis, or as a "package." You can save costs by doing some of the work yourself.

The various legal forms include the for-profit corporation, the partnership, the nonprofit corporation and the workers' cooperative. Look at the responsibilities and advantages of each form, and decide which seems best for your collective. We've also included information about getting tax-exempt status at the end of this section.

**For Profit Corporation**

This is the way most traditional businesses are set up. Corporations can be large or small. They can be strict or very loose and personal. As the author of "Small Time Operator" says, "Just as there are grey-suits-and-elevators corporations, there are bluejeans-and-pure-funk corporations."

The corporation is owned and managed by people who buy shares in the business. Usually, the largest shareholder gets the most votes. If members of the collective are stockholders, then you need to decide what happens if one person leaves. Will new members have to buy their way in?

One way to deal with this is to sell shares for a very small amount of money, so people are basically members in name only. You could make shares available for one dollar each, allow each worker to buy only one share, and then restrict the sales to workers only. Selling shares this way will not raise enough money to fund your group, so you'll have to get money somewhere else. All profits can be returned to workers as wages. Any other profits you keep will be taxed.

Corporations are very simple to set up. There are some other important things for you to know about them. They must have a legally elected board of directors who meet and choose officers to run the business. Corporations have to pay social security and unemployment benefits to workers. They are liable for accidents that happen to their employees on the job, and must carry workers' compensation. They are also liable for debts and any results of negligence. Liability for negligence can be insured against, but it's up to you. However, the worker-owners are not personally responsible for the debts of the business.

## Partnerships

A partnership is the most informal kind of association. In a self-managed workplace, all the workers should be partners. If anyone leaves, the partnership has to be legally reorganized, and this can be a real pain.

You can create a partnership by a verbal agreement, but we don't recommend it. Writing things down reduces future misunderstandings and problems. A written agreement, signed by everyone, should include a statement of goals, how much each person contributes in cash, property and labor, how each person will share in profits and losses, how money can be withdrawn and paid out, and how to continue the business if someone leaves.

Partners in a business can write checks and pay bills for each other. Every person in a partnership is responsible for the acts of every other partner, including paying off old debts.

Partners draw wages from the business accounts and pay taxes as self-employed people – they cannot hire themselves as employees. This means they are not eligible for unemployment benefits if they stop working with the group. However, the partnership can hire other employees. These people have taxes and social security withheld from their paychecks and are eligible for unemployment compensation.

Partners, as self-employed people, can deduct many of their business related expenses from their income before they pay taxes and social security. Many collectives take the partnership route, since it is informal and flexible. It is close to the spirit of a collective. But, there are disadvantages, such as personal liability and ineligibility for unemployment benefits.

**Nonprofit Corporations**

A big advantage of nonprofit corporations (in some states they are called not-for-profit corporations) is that no one owns them. They are run by "officers" elected by the members of the corporation. This can mean the members of the collective, or whatever group is chosen. The bylaws must specify how new people join the group and how the officers are elected. In most states there has to be at least one meeting of the corporation each year. Laws for nonprofit organizations vary widely, so find out what the law is for your state.

Everyone who is paid is an employee. Profits stay in the business and are not taxed. They are usually used for wages or capital growth. Nonprofit groups can have work-study students work for them, and the government pays 80 percent of the salaries.

Nonprofit corporations have to have a "purpose" – like education, charity or health care. Before applying, the stated purpose of the organization should be carefully chosen. In many states, there are limits on what kind of work that can be. Being a nonprofit corporation is not the same as being tax-exempt, but you must be a nonprofit state corporation to apply for federal tax-exemption (which then exempts you from state and federal corporate taxes).

**Workers' Cooperatives**

The workers' cooperative offers some advantages to the self-managed business. It tends to protect the rights of the workers more than other legal forms, by making the workers more important than money. It has "cooperative" in its name, which may be desirable. Again, the laws vary widely from state to state – some states such as Massachusetts don't even allow cooperatives. Others only allow them to deal with food, agriculture and housing.

### Tax-Exemption

Tax-exempt status can be very valuable. It provides exemption from most corporate taxes (state, local and federal). Tax-deductible donations may be received, as well as foundation grants. No sales tax is paid in many states. The federal unemployment tax (about 2 percent of payroll) is not required, and workers don't lose anything as a result.

Usually the group must be performing an educational or charitable function, receive its support from the general public, and must only do a minimum of lobbying or supporting of political candidates or campaigns.

The IRS has a complex application form, and they will want to see a budget. A lawyer's help in completing this form is useful.

It would be hard for a food co-op, a bike repair group or a bakery to get tax exemption. That's because it's hard to show that these groups are primarily educational or charitable. A bike repair training program for addicts would not have a problem; same with a health clinic or a group doing environmental education.

Tax-exempt groups have the option of not paying social security. We don't advocate this, because workers in collectives will need the social security contributions to make them eligible for benefits later in life.

A similar option exists in some states with unemployment funds. Again, we suggest that collectives pay unemployment premiums, so that workers can collect benefits. And if you do not have unemployment compensation insurance, a worker may still collect. You would then have to pay, dollar for dollar, for what they collected.

Tax-exemption can take quite a long time to obtain. Many groups ask established tax-exempt groups to "front" for them and accept tax-deductible donations for them while the application is pending. This is perfectly legal.

# Appendix 2. Setting Prices for Goods & Services

If a collective intends to support itself and its members from the sale of products and services, it will have to develop a sensible pricing policy. Most collectives find themselves caught between needing to make enough money, and providing services cheaply and to lots of people. Too often collectives underestimate costs and undercharge. To avoid this problem, you should carefully prepare a budget in which you try to predict your income and expenses. You want to find a pricing system that meets your political and financial needs.

When you make up a budget, remember that salaries are only one expense. Others include benefits, rent, utilities and phone, publicity, legal fees, and fundraising costs. Distinguish between start-up costs, and the costs that will be ongoing. Don't be overly optimistic about your income. It will take time for your group to become known and trusted.

There are three ways to determine what price to charge. One is by the demand for your product or service, whatever people are willing to pay. Another is by competition, basing the cost on what other similar businesses are charging. The last is basing the price on what it costs you to make or deliver the goods and services. This is the way most collectives would probably choose, since it matches their ideals most closely. There are different ways that groups we know have charged people, based on this cost-oriented pricing.

One is where everyone is charged the same fixed rate. Some repair collectives have found that if they charge a labor rate of two times what they will pay themselves, they will break even. So, if workers are paid five dollars an hour for labor, customers should be charged ten dollars an hour. Commercial restaurants usually charge four times the cost of the food for each dish, so collective restaurants keep this in mind when setting prices.

Collectives can offer interesting innovations in pricing. A bookstore gave a 15 percent discount to people who did two hours of work for them every three months. Since the Bicycle Repair Collective wants people to learn how to repair their own bikes, they charge a low rate for helping people fix their own bikes.

Another option is the flexible fee system, or sliding scale. Ideally this will make it possible for lower income people to use the collective. One women's health center charges a flat rate for abortions, but charges for all other services on a suggested scale. Patients are given a sheet with a suggested donation for what they received, and an envelope for the donation. The group usually gets about 75 percent of the amount it suggests. A counseling center allows each counselor to set his or her own sliding scale. They also have a scholarship fund. Greenhouse, which teaches courses in humanistic psychology, charges people a fixed amount which is based on each person's income.

The other option is to undercharge on some services, and aim at making a profit on others. VSC would like to finance other programs on income from our publications. Red Sun Press subsidizes their publications program from their print business. This allows them to publish literature that could not be published elsewhere. Some collectives charge higher rates but raise money from foundations and the government to offer help to low income people.

There are many ways to organize a pricing system. We urge collectives to go talk to other collectives and businesses to find out realistic estimates for costs and incomes. Every type of business usually has a rule of thumb in pricing such as the examples given above. Knowing these guidelines will help you be realistic in your planning.

For example, VSC used to underprice our publications by quite a bit. In the early days people felt that they'd just charge a little extra. No one researched to discover that bookstores take 40 percent of the cover price and so on. By learning from other small publishing groups we have become more realistic in our prices for publications and much more self-supporting.

# Appendix 3. Bookkeeping

Many people are intimidated by bookkeeping. They see it as endless rows of meaningless figures. In fact, the basic principles are easy to learn. A simple, well organized bookkeeping system can be very helpful for a collective to keep track of how things are going and to plan for the future.

**The Purposes of Bookkeeping**

A bookkeeping system is, at worst, a necessary evil, drawing energy from activities that seem more productive. Yet, it can be an information system that plays a key role in the decision-making process of a collective.

You can't learn to become a bookkeeper by reading this appendix, but you can get an idea of what it's all about. (Don't be discouraged if you have difficulty understanding this appendix; this brief section cannot fully cover the subject.) It's best to get some help from an experienced person in formally setting up your organization's books. If you don't have a friend who can help, you might hire an accountant. You can also look into getting help from students from a business school, if there is one nearby. One or more people in the collective could take a course at the local adult education center in bookkeeping or accounting. Keeping a basic textbook around would also be helpful.

Some of the functions of a good bookkeeping system are explained below.

1. *Meeting government requirements.* Many reports, like social security reports, sales and tax returns, and unemployment tax returns are required by various government agencies. A book-

keeping system gives the information asked for in these reports.

2. *Controlling resources.* A bookkeeping system helps you control your assets such as cash and amounts people owe you, and helps to prevent losses. It prevents overpayments and double payments.

3. *Reporting operations.* The end product of a bookkeeping system is financial reporting. Reports can show how much your collective is actually worth (financially) at any given time, or over a given period.

4. *Facilitating decision making and planning.* Information from the books can be used for pricing decisions (e.g., what does the meal we're preparing really cost when all costs are considered?). It helps measure how much you can afford to pay yourselves, and how well you are operating within the limits of your budget. It also helps with planning future activities. The books reflect the past and the present, which gives you some guidelines for predicting the future.

## Establishing a Bookkeeping System

There are many different ways of setting up a system for your collective to keep books. Because there are lots of books written on the subject (which we'll mention later), we'll just explain here that there are several things about which you must keep records in a good bookkeeping system.

These include records of all the checks you write, all the expenses you have, all the money you owe, all the money you receive, and all the money owed to you. If you have a bank account, you need to keep track of that account.

Many collectives have failed because they never bothered to keep accurate records of their financial transactions, or were very loose about it. Bookkeeping is one of the things in traditional businesses that we need because it actually does serve an important purpose. You should get some official ledger books from a stationary store, which will become full of categories, figures and columns.

To learn what to write in those columns and ledgers, you can look at the following sources; *Small Time Operator* second edition, by Bernard Kamoroff (Laytonville, CA: Bell Springs Publishing, 1980); *Accounting – A Self-Instruction Guide to Procedures and Theories* by Martin Bluestone, available from Macmillan Publishing Co.; and several publications from the Small Business Administration. You can get lists of free publications and booklets for sale by writing to them in Washington D.C. 20416, and asking for pamphlets 115A and 115B.

# Appendix 4. Resource Places

I. Co-ops, Collectives, Communities

A. Technical Assistance and Information

1. Alternative Work Project/Project Work
490 Riverside Dr., Room 517
New York, NY 10027

This group does research to help alternative workplaces start and keep in touch with each other. Much of their work is local.

2. Center for Conflict Resolution
731 State St.
Madison, WI 53703

CCR provides consultation and training in topics like conflict resolution, group process, program planning and organizational skills. They also help new groups select organizational and decision-making structures. Their manual is listed in Appendix Five.

3. Citizen's Involvement Training Project
138 Hasbrouck Bldg., University of Massachusetts
Amherst, MA 01003

CITP does workshops and sells manuals about many issues, including fundraising, community organizing, using the media, group process and staff training. They have worked with neighborhoods, state and local governments, schools and alternative businesses.

4. Community Consulting Group
   P.O. Box 7216
   Austin, TX 78712

CCG does training, consulting and writing to help co-ops avoid repeating the same mistakes. Most of their work is with local food co-ops.

5. Community Economics, Inc.
   6529 Telegraph Ave.
   Oakland, CA 94609

This group does consulting on the financial and legal aspects of a worker-owned business.

6. Community Jobs Clearinghouse
   1520 16th St. NW
   Washington, D.C. 20036

This project provides information on national social change job opportunities and internships. They also publish a monthly newsletter of job listings and articles.

7. Conway Consulting Collective
   P.O. Box 181
   Conway, MA 01341

CCC consults social change groups about many issues, including education, planning, communication, legal structure, and management.

8. Institute for Cooperative Community
   299 Harvard Square Station
   Cambridge, MA 02138

The institute offers lectures and publications about small cooperative communities as a form of human settlement, such as the Israeli kibbutz.

9. Institute for Local Self-Reliance
   1717 18th St. NW
   Washington, D.C. 20009

This group helps urban dwellers develop community based and controlled energy programs.

10. Institute for New Enterprise Development
    17 Dunster St.
    Cambridge, MA 02138

INED helps people and groups with the business planning of new community based and worker-owned ventures.

11. Movement for a New Society
    4722 Baltimore Avenue
    Philadelphia, PA 19143

MNS is a network of small groups throughout the country working for social change nonviolently. They do training on many issues, such as group process, personal growth, organizing and campaign building, and oppression issues. They have many excellent publications, some of which are listed in the bibliography.

12. North American Students of Cooperation
    P.O. Box 7293
    Ann Arbor, MI 48107

NASCO offers training, consulting, and publications for co-ops about management. They also sponsor an annual conference.

13. National Self-Help Resource Center
    2000 S. St., N.W.
    Washington, D.C. 20009

This center works with neighborhood and consumer groups and schools to develop expertise in planning, networking, and community organizing.

14. New England Cooperative Training Institute
    384 Whalley Ave., #226
    New Haven, CT 06511

NECTI provides training and support for alternative workplaces in New England about democratic management, arts management and food co-ops.

15. New School for Democratic Management
    589 Howard St.
    San Francisco, CA 94108

NDSM offers training in the "hard skills" of running an alternative business: financing, accounting, marketing, and management. They travel all over the country doing workshops.

16. New Ways to Work
    457 Kingsley Ave.
    Palo Alto, CA 94301

This group helps people find meaningful work, or start their own alternative workplaces. They have listings of local alternative agencies.

B. Financial Assistance

1. Haymarket People's Fund
   120 Boylston St., Room 707
   Boston, MA 02116

This group offers money to small, local community based social change efforts, who don't have access to traditional funding sources. They only fund New England, but there are similar groups in other areas. These are:

Vanguard Publications Foundation
4111 24th St.
San Francisco, CA 94114

Liberty Hill Foundation
P.O. Box 1074
Venice, CA 90291

North Star Fund
1133 Broadway Suite 1427
New York, NY 10010

People's Fund
1427 Walnut St., 4th Fl.
Philadelphia, PA 19102

2. Institute for Community Economics
   639 Massachusetts Ave.
   Cambridge, MA 02139

The institute is a resource center for the community land trust movement. They have a community investment fund model to help alternative businesses get started or expand.

3. National Consumer Cooperative Bank
   2001 S. St., NW
   Washington, D.C. 20009

The bank is new, and provides loans and support services to co-ops all over the country.

4. Southern Cooperative Development Fund, Inc.
   P.O. Box 3885
   Lafayette, LA 70501

This group offers loans and help to co-ops and community groups in the Southern United States who cannot get funding elsewhere.

C. Support

1. Consumer Cooperative Alliance
c/o Cooperative Services, Inc.
7404 Woodward Ave.
Detroit, MI 48202

The alliance is an international forum of all kinds of consumer co-ops, which has an annual conference.

2. Cooperative League of the USA
1828 L. St., NW
Washington, D.C. 20036

The League is a national lobbying and support group for producer and consumer co-ops.

3. Federation of Southern Cooperatives
P.O. Box 95
Epes, AL 35460

This federation includes 100 co-ops in fourteen states, many of which involve farming.

II. Workplace Democracy Efforts

A. Association for Self-Management
1414 Spring Rd. NW
Washington, D.C. 20010

The association is a network of individuals and chapters sharing information about self-management efforts around the world. They publish a quarterly newsletter and sponsor conferences.

B. Center for Economic Studies
457 Kingsley Ave.
Palo Alto, CA 94305

The center does research on producer cooperatives in the United States, plant closings, and the need for education in workplace democracy.

C. Exploratory Project on Economic Alternatives
2000 P St. NW #515
Washington, D.C. 20036

The project publishes reports about the planning aspects of worker ownership. They are helping with the worker management of a major steel mill in Youngstown, Ohio.

D. Industrial Cooperatives Association
249 Elm St.
Somerville, MA 02144

ICA helps east coast firms convert to worker ownership. They usually work with groups of wokers left behind by plant closings.

E. People's Business Commission
1346 Connecticut Ave., NW
Washington, D.C. 20036

By publications and speaking activities, PBC challenges the abuses of corporate power and mobilizes public support for democratic alternatives to the present economic system.

III. Organizations around Specific Issues (National)

A. Center for Science in the Public Interest
1757 S St., NW
Washington, D.C. 20009

B. Center for the Study of Education and Politics
Box RRR, Wesleyan Station
Middletown, CT 06457

C. Community Development Credit Union
Institute of the National Center for Urban Ethnic Affairs
1521 16th St.
Washington, D.C. 20036

D. Federation of Egalitarian Communities
Box CM2
Tecumseh, MO 65760

E. Gray Panthers
3700 Chestnut St.
Philadelphia, PA 19104

F. Liberation News Service
17 W. 17th St.
New York, NY 10011

G. National Alternative Schools Program
School of Education
University of Massachusetts
Amherst, MA 01003

H. National Association for Gardening
180 Flynn
Burlington, VT 05401

I. National Association of Housing Cooperatives
1828 L St., NW
Washington, D.C. 20036

J. National Association of Neighborhoods
1901 Que St., NW
Washington, D.C. 20009

K. National Center for Appropriate Technology
3040 Continental Drive (Box 3838)
Butte, MT 59701

L. National Community Land Trust Center
639 Massachusetts Ave.
Cambridge, MA 02139

M. National Council of La Raza
1725 I St., NW, Suite 210
Washington, D.C. 20006

N. National Federation of Community Broadcasters
1000 Eleventh St., NW
Washington, D.C. 20001

O. National Indian Youth Council
201 Hermosa, NE
Albuquerque, NM 87108

P. National Land for People
2348 N. Cornelia
Fresno, CA 93711

Q. National Lawyers Guild
23 Cornelia St.
New York, NY 10016

R. National Solar Heating and Cooling Information Center
Rockville, MD 20850
800-523-2929

S. National Training and Information Center
1123 W. Washington Blvd.
Chicago, IL 60607

T. New American Movement
3244 N. Clark St.
Chicago, IL 60657

U. NOW (National Organization for Women)
5 South Wabash, Suite 1615
Chicago, IL 60603

V. Quaker Project on Community Conflict
15 Rutherford Place
New York, NY 10003

W. Rural America
Dupont Circle Building
Washington, D.C. 20036

IV. Educational Programs

A. Cooperative College of Canada
141 105th West
Saskatoon, Saskatchewan S7NIN3

This is a cooperative college, offering courses in the business management of co-ops.

B. Program on Participation and Labor-Managed Systems
Uris Hall, Cornell University
Ithaca, NY 14853

This program offers a Ph.D., and is under the direction of Jaroslav Vanek. There is also a documentation center with resources.

C. Program in Social Economy and Social Policy
Department of Sociology
Boston College
Chestnut Hill, MA 02167

This is a new degree program to train trainers able to work on quality of working life, worker participation, and other workplace democratization programs.

# Appendix 5. Bibliography

Bernstein, Paul and Lew Bowers. "Democratic organization and management," *Communities*, No. 29, 1977, pp. 26-39.

This informative and easy-to-read article contains lots of practical ideas about running a collective. Some of them were included in chapters of this book. It covers such topics as planning, decision making, hirings, salaries and meetings. The article is based on their teachings at the New School for Democratic Management.

Case, John and Rosemary Taylor. *Coops, Communes and Collectives; Experiments in Social Change in the 1960's and 1970's*, New York: Pantheon Books, 1979.

An excellent collection of articles about the theory and practice of these "experiments." Part One deals with cases, including a free medical clinic, a free school, a food co-op and a law collective. Part Two raises issues, such as inequality between people, what makes alternatives work, and the prospects for American Socialism.

Center for Conflict Resolution. *A Manual for Group Facilitators*, Madison, WI: Center for Conflict Resolution, 1977.

This is a great introductory guide to group process, leading a group, running meetings and workshops, and basically helping things go smoothly in a group.

Communities, Journal of Cooperative Living. *A Guide to Cooperative Alternatives*, New Haven: Community Publications Cooperative, 1979.

This is *the* resource guide to thousands of groups in the country doing work in alternative agencies. Topics cover a wide range, including health, economics, food, housing, energy, culture, education, family life and relationships, and politics. Each chapter has an article about a sample group on that subject. This is how to reach other people doing what you're interested in.

Coover, Virginia, Ellen Deacon, Charles Esser and Christopher Moore. *Resource Manual for a Living Revolution*, Philadelphia: New Society Press, 1977.
This is a well organized, detailed book full of information about working for social change through nonviolent means. Covers political theory, working in groups, community organizing, sample workshops, and organizing demonstrations.

Freeman, Jo, "The Tyranny of Structurelessness," Berkeley *Journal of Sociology*, No. 17, 1972-73, pp. 151-64.
This article goes into more detail than what's presented in chapter seven of this book. It's one every collective should read before falling into the trap.

Holleb, Gordon P. and Walter H. Abrams. *Alternatives in Community Mental Health*, Boston: Beacon Press, 1975.
This book reviews the history of five drop-in counseling centers in eastern Massachusetts over a period of several years. It's interesting and mostly worth reading for the last chapter, which pulls everything together and presents an "Organizational Life Cycle" of development.

Ithaca Work Group. *Democracy in the Workplace: Readings on the Implementation of Self-Management in America*, Washington, D.C.: Strongforce, Inc., 1977.
Although not specifically written for or about collectives, this manual contains helpful information about working untraditionally. Topics include organizational structure, legal and tax requirements, marketing, and finance.

Lyons, Gracie. *Constructive Criticism: A Handbook*, Oakland CA: Issues in Radical Therapy Press, 1974.
A how-to book on giving and receiving criticism, mixed in with radical economics and politics. The back cover says it "will increase the power of people's work as well as their personal sense of well

being and satisfaction... an excellent tool for peaceful Revolution."

Training/Action Affinity Group, ed. *Building Social Change Communities*, Philadelphia: Movement for a New Society, 1979.

This guide is full of information for people in the social change movement. Chapters deal with communal living, consensus, running meetings, relationships, conflict resolution, and networks. Written for people living together, but most of it applies to people working together as well.

Woodrow, Peter. *Clearness-Processes for Supporting Groups and Individuals in Decision Making*, Philadelphia: Movement for a New Society, 1976.

An easy to read pamphlet explaining a process for helping make choices. Can be done with people wanting to get some direction about their life and work, or used as a process for accepting (or not accepting) new members in groups. This method has been used successfully at Movement for a New Society for years.

**Other Books**

American Friends Service Committee/Simple Living Collective. *Taking Charge: Achieving Personal and Political Change through Simple Living*. New York: Bantam Books, 1977.

Co-op Handbook Collective. *The Food Coop Handbook*, 1975.

French, David and Elaine French. *Working Communally: Patterns and Possibilities*. New York: Russell Sage Foundation, 1975.

Gowan, Suzanne, Georgy Lakey, William Moyer, and Richard Taylor. *Moving Toward a New Society*. Philadelphia: New Society Press, 1976.

*Journal of Applied Behavioral Sciences*. "Special Issue on Alternative Institutions." Vol. 9, Nos. 2-3, 1973.

Kanter, Rossabeth M. *Commitment and Community: Communes and Utopias in Sociological Perspective*. Cambridge, MA: Harvard University Press, 1972.

Lakey, George. *Strategy for a Living Revolution*. San Francisco: Freeman Press, 1973.

Kokopeli, Bruce and George Lackey. *Leadership for Change*. Philadelphia: Movement for a New Society, 1978.

Macro-Analysis Collective. *Organizing Macro-Analysis Seminars: A Manual.* Philadelphia: Movement for a New Society, 1975.

Negrin, Su. *Begin at Start: Some Thoughts on Personal Liberation and World Change.* New York: Times Change Press, 1972.

Red Sunshine Gang. *Anti-Mass.* New York: Come Unity Press.

Rosenberg, Marshall. *From Now On: Without Blame or Punishment.* St. Louis: Community Psychological Consultants, Inc., 1977.

Sarason, Seymour B. *The Creation of Settings and the Future Societies.* San Francisco: Jossey-Bass, 1972.

Satin, Mark. *New Age Politics: Healing Self and Society.* West Vancouver, B.C.: Whitecap Books, 1978.

Vanguard Public Foundation. *Robin Hood Was Right: A Guide to Giving Your Money for Social Change.* San Francisco: Vanguard Foundation, 1977.

**Further Readings on Workplace Management**

Bernello, George and Dimitrious Roussopoulos. *The Case for Participatory Democracy.* New York: Grossman Publishers, 1971.

Bernstein, Paul. *Workplace Democratization: It's Internal Dynamics.* Kent, OH: Kent State University Press, 1976.

Carnoy, Martin and Derek Shearer. *Economic Democracy: The Challenge of the 1980s.* White Plains, NY: M.E. Sharpe, Inc., 1980.

Davis, Louis E. and Albert B. Cherns: *The Quality of Working Life.* New York: The Free Press, 1975.

Dolgoff, Sam. *The Anarchist Collectives: Worker's Self-Management in the Spanish Revolution 1936-1939.* New York: Free Life Edition, 1974.

Herbst, Phillip G. *Alternatives to Hierarchies.* Lieden, Netherlands: H.E. Stenfert Kroese, 1976.

Hunnius, Gerry C., David Carson, and John Case, Eds. *Worker's Control: A Reader on Labor and Social Change.* New York: Vintage Books, 1973.

Oakeshott, Robert. *The Case for Worker's Coops.* London: Rouldedge and Kegan Press, 1978.

Schumacher, E.F. *Small is Beautiful: Economics as if People Mattered.* New York: Harper and Row, 1973.

Vanek, Jaroslav. *Self-Management: Economic Liberation of Man.* Baltimore: Penguin Books, 1975.

Zwerdling, Daniel. *Workplace Democracy: A Guide to Workplace Ownership, Participation and Self-Management Experiments in the United States and Europe.* New York: Harper and Row, 1978. 1978.

## Periodicals

*Akwesasne Notes*
Rooseveltown, NY 13683
This is the journal of Native American Peoples, which includes art poetry, and information.

*Changing Men*
Men's Resource Center
3534 SE Main
Portland, OR 97214
This is a bi-monthly publication whose aim is to spread the word about anti-sexist men.

*Co-Evolution Quarterly*
P.O. Box 428
Sausalito, CA 94965
The quarterly continues the work of the *Whole Earth Catalogue*, by doing book reviews and articles on a variety of "new age" topics.

*Communities: Journal of Cooperative Living*
P.O. Box 426G
Louisa, VA 23093
*Communities* is a bi-monthly journal published by and for people involved in cooperative life.

*Community Jobs Newsletter*
1520 16th St. NW
Washington, D.C. 20036
This monthly newsletter provides information on and access to social change career opportunities throughout the United States.

*Country Women Magazine*
P.O. Box 208
Albion, CA 95410
This is a collectively run feminist magazine which publishes works by women – articles, poetry, graphics and photographs.

*Dollars and Sense*
324 Somerville Ave.
Somerville, MA 02143
This monthly magazine analyzes the U.S. economy in a way that everyone can understand. They believe that private enterprise is the source and not the solution of our problems.

*In These Times*
1509 N. Milwaukee Ave.
Chicago, IL 60622
*In These Times* is an independent socialist weekly offering in-depth coverage of the nation and the world.

*Medical Self-Care*
Access to Medical Tools
P.O. Box 717
Inverness, CA 94937
This magazine helps consumers take more responsibility for their own health.

*Mother Jones*
1255 Portland Place
Boulder, CO 80302
This popular magazine has well-written articles on politics, environment, health and the arts.

*New Age Magazine*
32 Station St.
Brookline, MA 02146
*New Age* is a monthly magazine about new ideas and lifestyles, emphasizing health, environment, human potential and consciousness issues.

*Off Our Backs*
1724 20th St.
Washington, D.C. 20009
This is a monthly women's news journal covering a variety of issues.

*Self-Reliance*
1717 18th St. NW
Washington, D.C. 20009
This newsletter reports on communities' efforts to become more self-sufficient and politically independent.

*Ways and Means*
Conference/Alternative State and Local Policies
1901 Que St.
Washington, D.C. 20009
This bi-monthly publication focuses on major issues facing state and local government.

*Win*
503 Atlantic Avenue, 5th Floor
Brooklyn, NY 11217
*Win* is a bi-weekly magazine for peace and freedom through nonviolent action. It is published with the support of the War Resisters League.

*Working Papers for a New Society*
4 Nutting Road
Cambridge, MA 02138
This bi-monthly magazine focuses on new political ideas and reform movements.

## Other publications from
## VOCATIONS FOR SOCIAL CHANGE

Vocations for Social Change (VSC) was started in the fall of 1970. For its first five years it was a collectively run program of the American Friends Service Committee. The original goal of VSC was to help people find work that contributed to meaningful, constructive social change and personal fulfillment. In addition, VSC has helped hundreds of organizing and social change groups find dedicated and committed people to carry on their work. VSC continues to operate a small resource center for this purpose.

During its history, VSC has run counseling programs, the Unemployment Law Project, and the Labor Information Project. VSC has also provided technical assistance to collectives and co-ops, and a campus workshop program entitled "Finding Work for Social Change."

VSC publishes and distributes social change publications. The following titles are available from VSC. (Note: Prices in parenthesis are for institutions.)

1980-81 **Boston People's Yellow Pages** at $5.70 ($6).

**How to Get a Job in Boston**, 3rd Ed. at $4.75 ($5.25).

**Legal Tactics:** Hand book for Mass. Tenants at $5.75 ($6.50).

**Your Rights as a Worker** at $2 ($2.50).

**Why Do We Spend So Much Money** at $2.50 ($3).

**What's Happening to Our Jobs** at $3 ($3.50).

The following titles, available from VSC, were written by the Citizen Involvement Training Project:

**Power: A Repossession Manual**; Organizing Strategies for Citizens at $6.75 ($7.25).

**Planning, for a Change**: A Citizen's Guide to Creative Planning Program Development at $6.75 ($7.25).

**The Rich Get Richer and the Poor Write Proposals** at $6.75 ($7.25).

**Playing Their Game Our Way**: Using the Political Process to Meet Community Needs at $6.75 ($7.25).

**We Interrupt This Program...** A Citizen's Guide to Using the Media for Social Change at $6.75 ($7.25).

**How to Make Citizen Involvement Work** at $6.75 ($7.25).

**Working Together:** A Manual to Help Groups Work More Effectively at $6.75 ($7.25).

**Beyond Experts:** A Guide for Citizen Group Training at $6.75 ($7.25).

All orders should be prepaid. We'd also be glad to send you a more complete publications brochure.

Vocations For Social Change
PO Box 211, Essex Station
Boston, MA 02112

**Reflections of a Rock Lobster: A story about growing up gay** $4.95
by Aaron Fricke

Guess who's coming to the prom! No one in Cumberland, Rhode Island, was surprised when Aaron Fricke appeared at his high school prom with a male date. He had sued his school for the right to do so, and the media had been full of the news.

Yet for the first sixteen years of his life, Fricke had closely guarded the secret of his homosexuality. *Reflections of a Rock Lobster* is his story about growing up with this secret. With insight and humor, Fricke tells how he first became aware of his homosexual feelings in childhood, then learned to hide them from adults, and then to repress his feelings completely, before he finally developed a positive gay identity. '*Rock Lobster* is simply the most realistic, revealing, painful, insightful and – finally – joyful story about growing up gay in America that you will ever read.' (*New York Native.*)

**Young, Gay and Proud** $2.95

One high school student in ten is gay. Here is the first book ever to address the problems and needs of that often-invisible minority, helping young people deal with questions like: Am I really gay? What would my friends think if I told them? Should I tell my parents? Does anybody else feel the way I do?

**Energy, Jobs and the Economy** $3.45
by Richard Grossman and Gail Daneker

Sure you're in favor of solar energy. But what about your Uncle Joe, who's worried that without nuclear power we'll have blackouts and plant closings and that he may lose his job? This highly readable book shows that solar and renewable energy sources are not only safer than nuclear power, they're also better for the economy and for working people.

**Health Care for the People: Studies from Vietnam** $6.95
by Dr. Joan McMichael

This account of medical services in Vietnam will inspire everyone who believes that a humane health system is indeed possible. Organized in the face of enormous adversity, the Vietnamese system puts to shame the medical establishments of many far more "developed" countries.

Ask for these titles in your bookstore. If unavailable locally, you may order them (as well as more copies of *No Bosses Here!* directly from Alyson Publications, Dept. B15, PO Box 2783, Boston, MA 02208. Please enclose full payment with your order and add 75¢ postage on orders for one book. (If you order two or more books, we'll pay postage.)